LOBSTERS great & small

HOW SCIENTISTS AND FISHERMEN ARE CHANGING OUR UNDERSTANDING OF A MAINE ICON

386 Main Street
Post Office Box 648
Rockland, Maine 04841
www.islandinstitute.org

Editor: David Platt
Design & Production: Paige Garland Parker
Photography: ©Peter Ralston, ©Nick Caloyianis
Map Graphics: Chris Brehme
Research and Additional Writing: Leslie Fuller, Ben Neal and Nakomis Nelson
Additional Design Elements: Jose Conde, Studio Pepin
Printing: J.S. McCarthy, Augusta, ME
Distributed by DownEast Books, Camden, ME

Front Cover Photo: ©Peter Ralston
Back Cover Photo: ©Nick Caloyianis

MAP: CHRIS BREHME AFTER MODEL BY E. ROWORTH AND R. SIGNELL, USGS

dedication

To the fishermen and scientists of the Gulf of Maine working to sustain the region's fishing heritage

Jamie Wyeth, *Buoy Tree,* 1991

table of contents

PETER RALSTON

foreword

By Senator Olympia J. Snowe

Maine, for many, has become synonymous with one word: lobster.

While our nickname may be "The Pine Tree State," it is *Homarus americanus* that has become legend, a way of life, and a source of both jobs and pride for the people of Maine.

This rugged and storied industry not only helps define us as a people, but is also a powerful economic engine, returning an estimated $227 million to our economy, employing 22,000 directly and supporting families and communities all along Maine's famed, rocky coast. Clearly, the management of this precious resource has profound implications not only for the lobster, but also for the future of our state. It is therefore in everyone's best interest that decisions affecting the harvest of lobsters be based on a comprehensive assessment of the best information available.

In that light, I especially appreciate the collaborative efforts represented by the studies chronicled in this book. The reality is that any ecosystem as incredibly complex as Penobscot Bay requires an assessment that is equally multi-faceted, involving all affected stakeholders. So when a group from the Island Institute approached me in my capacity as Chair of the U.S. Senate Subcommittee on Oceans and Fisheries in 1996, I was proud to pair them with a federal agency that keeps data collected by our nation's satellites. The Institute wanted to better understand Penobscot Bay's intricate marine environment and, as it happened, the agency was looking for practical applications for the information it gathered. The resulting marriage produced an innovative means of placing one more piece of the oceanographic puzzle.

Maine has been a pioneer in developing and adopting responsible lobster harvesting rules, and it is only natural that we should once again be at the forefront. As this book will demonstrate, "Dirigo" or, "I lead", continues to be an entirely appropriate motto for the State of Maine, and I hope the effort detailed in this book will serve as a model for future research in Maine, the United States and throughout the world.

Olympia Snowe

introduction

By H. Lee Dantzler, Director
National Oceanographic Data Center
NOAA/NESDIS

Satellites have long been used to support weather forecasting, land mapping and large-scale oceanographic research. Their routine use in coastal marine resources management, however, has been limited for several reasons. Most satellites were unable to resolve the important small-scale physical and biological features in coastal waters. A substantial (and costly) communications and computing infrastructure was generally required to handle the high data volumes that imaging satellites typically produce. And the satellite data analysis software needed to extract useful information from the imagery was technically complex and generally the domain of universities and major research laboratories.

The explosive growth in the 1990s in digital communications, Internet, computing and satellite data processing technologies, as well as corresponding increases in satellite sensing capabilities promised to change all this. Consequently, in 1996, the Ocean Remote Sensing Program of NOAA's National Environmental Satellite, Data, and Information Service embarked on a major five-year demonstration project to determine whether environmental satellite data could be practically and cost effectively used at the state level to support coastal marine resources management. The project faced many challenges. For example, could environmental satellite data processing and distribution services that were historically sized for global and national environmental monitoring requirements be "right sized" for routine state and regional coastal uses that vary from region to region? Living marine resource management is complex. How can these complexities be constrained to afford a realistic test? Most important, how could a co-equal partnership among federal, state, private, industry and nonprofit stakeholders in the selected region be established to ensure the end user's involvement, as well as an objective evaluation?

Maine's Penobscot Bay region was selected as the test site for this demonstration, originally called the Penobscot Bay Marine Resources Collaborative Project. This choice was driven by several factors. Penobscot Bay is home to the most productive coastal commercial fishery (lobster) in the northeastern United States, a fishery that was facing important management issues. The physical and biological ecosystem scales were right to evaluate the use of satellite data, while small enough to be tractable. A partnership of interested and actively supportive state agencies, public and private universities, commercial fishing industry organizations, and nonprofit organizations involved in coastal marine resources management issues was immediately possible.

This book outlines the basis, activities, and successful outcomes of this novel effort. It was successful in many ways as a result of the commitment and active support of the contributing organizations to the project. Of these, a particular note of thanks is given to the Maine State Planning Office, which led the partnership advisory council for the project; and to the Island Institute of Rockland, Maine, which provided early in-state leadership in helping to launch the effort. The Institute provided indispensable assistance throughout the project as a "partnership facilitator" within the state. Without the support of these and all the participants, this effort would not have been possible.

National Oceanic and Atmospheric Administration, National Environmental Satellite, Data, and Information Service, 1335 East-West Highway, Silver Spring, MD 20910

PETER RALSTON

LOBSTERS
great & small
HOW SCIENTISTS AND FISHERMEN ARE CHANGING
OUR UNDERSTANDING OF A MAINE ICON

PETER RALSTON

1

Hauling Together

THE CENTER OF THE LOBSTER UNIVERSE

THIS IS A STORY ABOUT COOPERATION and collaboration in the Maine lobster fishery. Between 1996 and 2001, over 150 fishermen joined with a dozen different scientists from five research institutions, three local non-profits, three state agencies and the federal government's chief ocean management organization to investigate the health and future of the lobster resource in Penobscot Bay, Maine. This collaboration is a model for how complex and contentious fishery problems can be understood and resolved at a time when fisheries resources are threatened in all oceans of the globe.

Before long the agencies and organizations would be joined by other lobster fishermen and a hardy band of young interns, all working together aboard the fishermen's boats and in laboratories to gather and interpret data for what would become known as the Penobscot Bay Collaborative.

The collective efforts of all these individuals and institutions brought the knowledge of American lobsters, their breeding habits and their habitats to a new level, making it likely for the first time in the three-century history of this unusual, conservation-minded fishery that its future productivity can be reliably predicted.

While high technology was a crucial player - investigators worked with underwater sidescan sonar, radar, satellites, sensors attached to automated buoys and the latest in mapping and geographic information systems (GIS) - the project's diverse collaborations were even more important to its success. Over five years, the work of the Penobscot Bay Collaborative ultimately involved many times more fishermen than scientists. It achieved scientific breakthroughs, but its real legacy is

Penobscot Bay, Maine is the center of abundance of the American lobster. No place else in the entire North Atlantic range of the lobster are there higher concentrations of this most valuable crustacean. The question of whether lobsters are being overfished or not has fueled a raging debate between lobstermen and scientists who came together for the first time in a five year long project to seek answers.

the successful collaboration of so many players.

Maine Lobsters' Global Reach For much of the past half century, the market for Maine lobsters has been limited largely to the period between the 4th of July and Labor Day, a time when they they have shed their old shells, but before their new ones have hardened. From a business point of view, the summer selling season is a terrible proposition. The soft-shelled lobsters are vulnerable to all kinds of stresses and cannot be transported much beyond New England, restricting demand. Meanwhile, everyone is catching lots of lobsters, so there is an abundant supply. Year in and year out, the equation of high supply and restricted markets has spelled out the same result: depressed prices and angry lobstermen with no alternatives but to sell soft product into a soft market.

But slowly, over the past decade and a half, a revolution of sorts has transformed this industry. More sophisticated methods of holding lobsters in pounds have been developed by dealers willing to take the risk of storing a perishable product for fall and winter, when prices might increase. Year by year, markets have expanded - first into southern and midwestern markets, then into the far corners of the continental United States.

Now the development of new air shipping containers and methods has trans-

PETER RALSTON

During the last decade wooden lobster traps such as these on Criehaven Island and Port Clyde (facing page) have been almost entirely replaced by new vinyl-coated wire traps.

formed the Maine lobster into a global commodity. Big markets for lobsters from Penobscot Bay and other regions of the Maine coast have developed in London, Paris and Berlin. The West Coast of the United States today is no longer a long haul for lobster dealers; today the far edge of the market for live Maine lobsters is Japan and the Far East. In 1999, on the eve of the British departure from Hong Kong, 4,000 pounds of lobsters from Vinalhaven, Maine, were shipped by air to mark the occasion. Everyone in the world, it seems, recognizes the Maine lobster as a premium seafood.

Center of Abundance Rockland, Maine, promotes itself as the "Lobster Capital of the World." The town's annual Lobster Festival has grown from a celebration of local pride into a national event. Over 100,000 visitors throng Rockland's streets for the three-day event, which still features the crowning of a local beauty as the festival's Sea Goddess. Over 50,000 lobsters are served. One year, the festival even attracted the notice of People for the Ethical Treatment of Animals (PETA), which symbolically released a large adult lobster into Penobscot Bay.

Recent scientific findings provide some basis in fact for Rockland's self-proclaimed status. Biologists have shown that the density of lobster populations at a handful of locations in Penobscot Bay are among the highest recorded anywhere in the entire North Atlantic range of *Homarus americanus*.

But more than Rockland depends on lobsters. Over 1,500 lobstermen from East Penobscot Bay towns such as Stonington and Deer Isle, from the island communities of Vinalhaven and Matinicus and from Owls Head, Sprucehead and Tenants Harbor along the western shores of the bay all depend on this species' annual cycle of abundance.

In recent years, we have become accustomed to stories of marine resource depletion, particularly the disheartening collapse of Atlantic cod on the Grand Banks of Newfoundland and Georges Bank at the southern edge of the Gulf of Maine. A glance at the lobster pot buoys in July on the surface of any cove or bay in Maine—which from a distance look like confetti after a New York City parade—makes one wonder whether lobsters will go the way of cod and so many other resources that have been fished to the brink of commercial extinction.

To understand whether the lobster resource can withstand the

PETER RALSTON

HOW THE CONSERVATION ETHIC DEVELOPED

Penobscot Bay lobster fishermen insist that the reason lobster populations have been able to withstand the intense harvest pressure to which they are subject is the lobsterman's conservation ethic. They are proud that Maine lobster fishermen have evolved a set of protections for young lobsters and females that keeps the reproductive potential of the population healthy.

Some of Maine's first marine resource protection laws were enacted over a century ago to protect young lobsters. In 1887, after a divisive battle, the Maine Legislature enacted a law to prohibit landing "short" lobsters less than 10 inches in overall length. Later the law was modified to make it more uniform and enforceable so that the minimum size that could be harvested was based on carapace length—the length of the shell from behind a lobster's eye socket to the beginning of its tail. But the intent was the same: to protect young lobsters so they could lay eggs at least once before it was legal to harvest them.

The initial lobster conservation law was controversial and widely ignored. Beginning in the 1930s, however, lobsters became increasingly scarce and landings declined. Lobstermen began, as a matter of necessity, to observe the conservation law to protect short lobsters. Offenders were reported to Sea and Shore Fisheries wardens for the first time, and the Department's Commissioner, Horatio Crie (who came from a lobstering family that founded the island fishing community of Criehaven) began prosecuting the cheaters. At the end of the 1930s, dealers pressed the Legislature for an additional law to prohibit the landing of large lobsters. Although it was billed as a conservation measure to protect "broodstock" lobsters, most observers recognized that the primary motive was economic. Dealers simply couldn't sell lobsters that exceeded two or three pounds in weight to consumers, and didn't want to be forced to buy them from lobstermen.

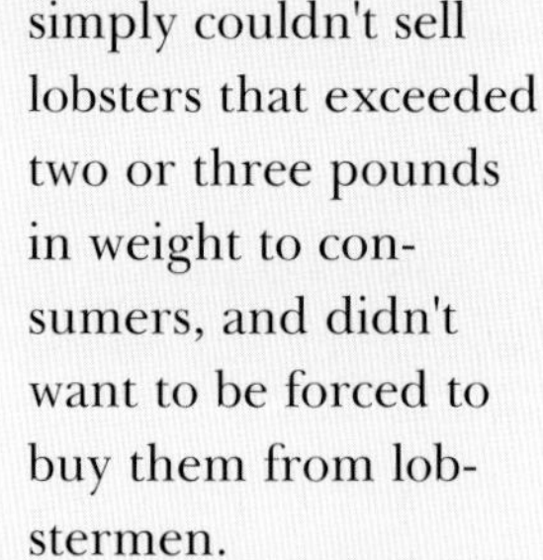

The Legislature passed a prohibition on landing oversize lobsters, and thus was born Maine's "double-gauge" lobster law protecting both juveniles and large adults.

The effect of these laws is to concentrate the harvest on "chicken lobsters," ideally weighing between a pound and a quarter and a pound and a half, the size best suited to a lobster dinner. But

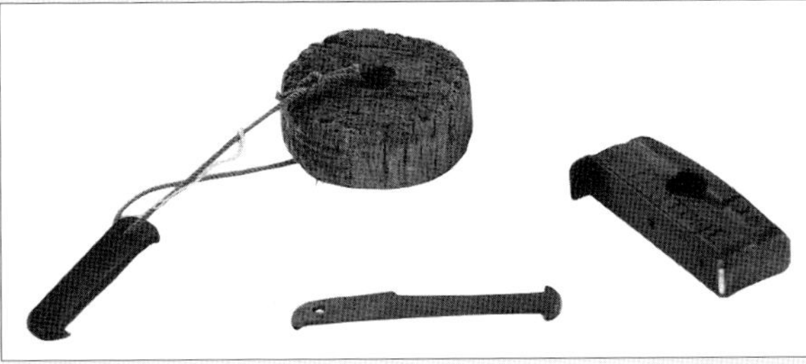

the important biological effect was to protect large egg-producing females and their mates.

The next major lobster conservation rule developed informally from grassroots common sense. Because female lobsters carry their eggs externally on the undersides of their tails for almost a year as they develop, egg-bearing lobsters are immediately recognizable. Beginning in the 1960s and spreading slowly from harbor to harbor, lobstermen began to mark egg-bearing females with a "V-notch" on one of their tail flippers and returning them to the water where they could release their eggs. This practice not only protects a female lobster during the period when she carries her eggs, but the notch lasts for several molts of her shell, often until she is protected by the oversize measure, and lobstermen thus began returning V-notched females to the water whether or not they were carrying eggs at the time. Although official protection of V-notch lobsters became law in 1938, it wasn't enforced until pressure from lobstermen began to increase in the 1970s and 80s.

The passage of these and other laws represents the gradual spread of a lobster conservation ethic among lobster fishermen. Lobstermen were no more noble than other fishermen, but they have always been more vigilant about who is (and who is not) playing by the rules. The rules that regulate the Maine lobster fishery are a contrast to the oft-cited "tragedy of the commons" scenario, where fishermen compete to catch the last fish on the basis of the belief that if "I don't catch the last fish, the next guy will." In the lobster fishery, participants enforce their own rules and cheaters are dealt with summarily by the lobstermen themselves. A person who breaks the rules by selling shorts, scrubbing the eggs off females or taking oversized lobsters to boil and sell the meat may find his gear cut off or his boat damaged. Jim Acheson, who has studied the Maine lobster fishery for decades, has termed the conservation ethic "mutual coercion, mutually enforced." (PC)

Early lobster gauge measures (top) and cedar lobster pot buoys

COURTESY OF MAINE MARITIME MUSEUM

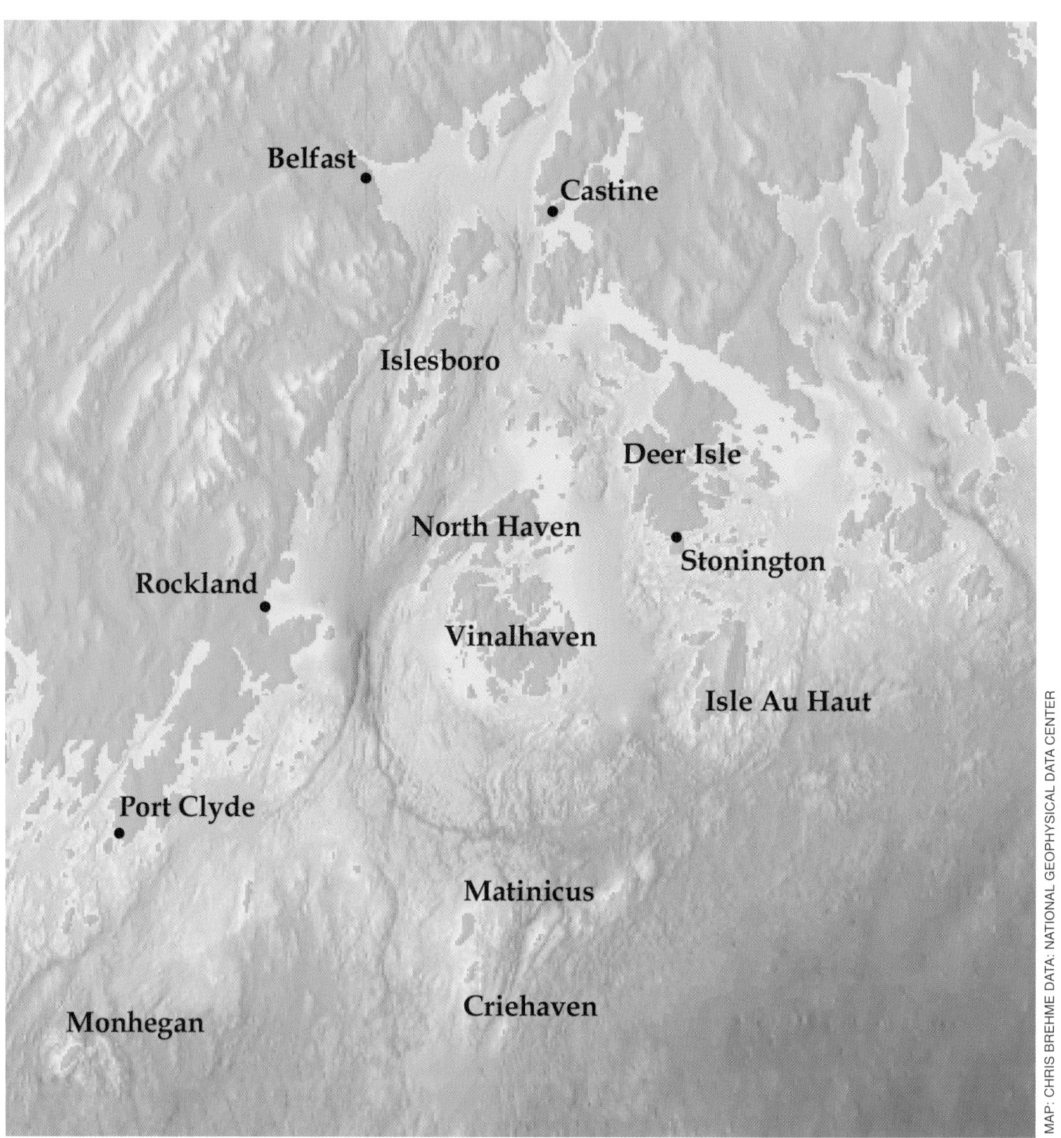

MAP: CHRIS BREHME DATA: NATIONAL GEOPHYSICAL DATA CENTER

Lobster towns ring the rim of Penobscot Bay and are the critical economic underpinning for the island communities of North Haven, Vinalhaven, Isle au Haut, Criehaven, Matinicus and Monhegan.

pressure of the current exploitation and harvest rates, scientists and lobstermen need to understand why there are so many lobsters in a place like Penobscot Bay.

Many Lobsters, Many Opinions There's a saying in the region: ask two lobstermen why there are so many lobsters in the bay, and you get three different answers.

It's a fact that something almost unheard-of in marine fisheries has occurred in the Maine lobster fishery. For the 40 years between 1948 and 1988, this fishery rarely varied more than 10 percent, plus or minus, from a yearly harvest level of 20 million pounds. It was one of the few fisheries that appeared to be stable year in and year out. But in the late1980s, lobster harvests in Maine began to tick upward. Year by year, landings increased by several million pounds. By the mid-1990s

Clockwise from top: knitting the 'heads' that allow lobsters to enter a trap but not escape; filling bait bags with a baiting iron; making bait with redfish 'racks' off Criehaven Island.

PETER RALSTON (3)

Maine lobster landings had more than doubled, exceeding 40 million pounds. And landings continued to increase each year, breaking century-old landings records, until they peaked at almost 57 million pounds in 2000. How could this be? Of course, abundance recorded only as landings is also related to changes in harvesting technology, lobster regulations and market factors. Nevertheless, many indices of lobster population trends indicate there has been an absolute increase in the number of lobsters on the bottom along the coast of Maine and elsewhere in the natural habitats of *Homarus americanus*.

To explain this abundance some lobstermen point to the conservation traditions of their fishery and a series of conservation tools, initiated by fishermen and now on the books as laws. Others cite the decline of cod, a predator. While the absence of cod may indeed be a contributing factor, it is difficult to conclude from the historic record that the dearth of cod alone is the driving force in the lobster increase of the last decade. Ted Ames, a Maine fisherman who interviewed old-time cod fishermen to understand the patterns of cod decline, found that these fish had largely disappeared from Penobscot Bay by the late 1940s, after their spawning grounds were first intensively targeted and harvested.

Bob Steneck, a lobster biologist from the University of Maine, and his colleague, Jim Acheson, argue that cod predation may have played a major role in the collapse of lobsters from the 1920s to 1930. During that time, landings records show, there were many large old cod in inshore areas of the coast, just as conservation laws protecting juvenile lobsters were beginning to take effect. Steneck and Acheson hypothesize that a large population of older cod, preying on a population of newly protected juvenile lobsters, could have resulted in the depressed lobster populations that characterized that period, despite practices aimed at increasing the abundance of lobsters.

But the cod predation theory does not explain why lobster populations did not begin to increase for another two to three decades after the disappearance of large spawning concentrations of cod and other groundfish in the 1940s and 50s.

It's also argued that the increasing amount of bait in the water from the proliferation of lobster traps feeds lobsters and explains their abundance. This idea, like the cod predation theory, doesn't necessarily square with the facts. While most scientists believe that the amount of bait in lobster traps in a place like Penobscot Bay can increase lobster growth rates and that the "aquaculture effect" of bait could theoretically explain an increase in growth and hence production, they maintain that bait alone is insufficient to explain the more-than-100-percent increase that has occurred. Simply stated, the lobsters had to survive before they could grow.

PETER RALSTON

Wooden buoys, once hand carved from Atlantic white cedar in a fish house during the long winter days , have now been replaced by inexpensive styrofoam buoys.

A 10-year study of the interaction of urchins and lobsters conducted by Steneck and others has pointed to a change in benthic (bottom) habitats in inshore areas of the Maine coast. In the late 1980s, the development and rapid growth of a Japanese market for green urchin roe resulted in the harvest of millions of pounds of urchin biomass in inshore areas. The removal of the urchins, which graze on kelp as their main food source, resulted in the rapid growth of kelp beds, in turn providing excellent protective cover for shedding lobsters. Still, Steneck does not believe the kelp beds are the whole story, especially since this explanation does not account for increases in landings in places where there are neither urchins nor kelp.

Finally, some scientists and fishermen wonder whether changes in sea temperatures and/or currents along the Maine coast have played a role in the rise in lobster harvests. Unfortunately, except for the Boothbay area, the comprehensive set of sea temperature records required to test this theory does not exist. Orbiting satellites have been collecting sea surface temperature readings, however, and offer a means of testing the theory that shifting currents and sea temperature changes may play a role in determining the abundance of lobsters. The relationship between ocean temperatures and currents and lobster abundance would become one of the major questions tested during the Penobscot Bay Collaborative's five-year study of lobster dynamics.

Data from the Skies In 1996 Maine Sen. Olympia Snowe, then the Chair of the U.S. Senate Subcommittee on Oceans and Fisheries, introduced a small group from the Island Institute to a federal agency that archives the nation's satellite data, the National Environmental Satellite Data and Information Service (NESDIS). The Institute was looking for help in applying satellite data to issues of coastal management. NESDIS is best known for operating the nation's network of weather satellites, but it is also responsible for another set of satellites capable of detecting sea surface temperatures around the globe. With enhanced access to their data, researchers could test the hypothesis that changing sea temperatures, and the distribution of temperatures, influence lobster distribution and abundance.

When satellites equipped with specialized infrared sensors pass over the world's oceans, it is possible to detect patterns and differences between warmer and cooler bodies of water. The satellites do not actually measure the temperature of seawater; one must still to go out and do that directly—but they can detect very small variations in the way warm and cold water reflect light off the ocean's surface. When

An adult lobster defending its territory with its sharp pincer claw (right) and its powerful crusher claw (left).

NICK CALOYIANIS

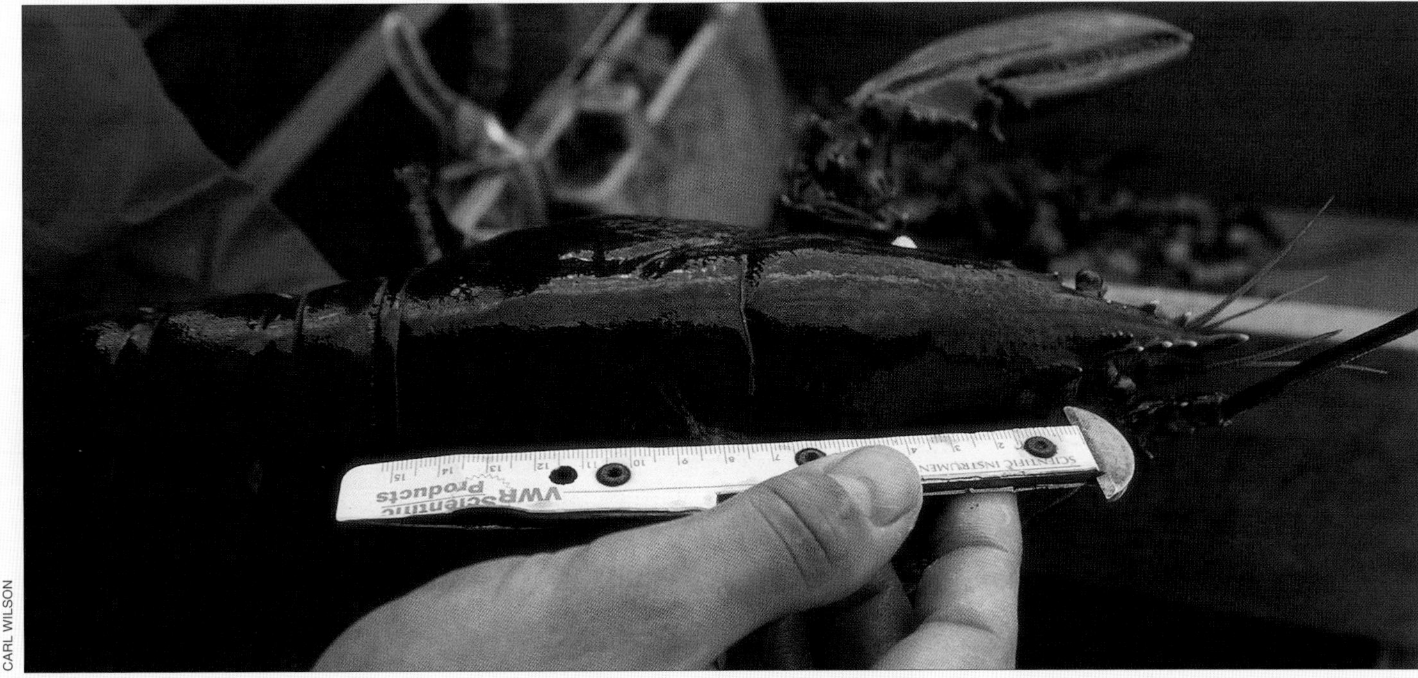

CARL WILSON

SAMPLING AT SEA

One of the problems lobster scientists have had in understanding the population dynamics of Maine's lobster fishery is that the statistics collected by state and federal regulators are based primarily on harvests. State and federal officials periodically survey lobstermen's catches to determine the number and sizes of males and females from the millions of lobsters landed each year, and from this information, they extrapolate a picture of the entire lobster population along the Maine coast. While this landings data provides crucial information on the status and trends in the lobster population, there is an inherent problem: no one gets a picture of how many oversized, V-notched females (which are protected under Maine law) are returned to the water. Nor do we get a picture of the number of smaller juveniles, presumably an indicator of future landings. To address these information gaps the Department of Marine Resources established a "sea sampling" program to collect information on the number, size, sex and other particulars of the lobsters fishermen catch in their traps and then return to the water. The program was limited in scope, however, and it didn't cover Penobscot Bay.

The Penobscot Bay Collaborative significantly enhanced Maine's sea sampling program. Carl Wilson, who had been a graduate student of lobster biologist Bob Steneck at the University of Maine, joined the Island Institute, where he coordinated and expanded the sea sampling program in Penobscot Bay and the surrounding region.

As part of the program, student interns periodically boarded the vessels of cooperating lobster fishermen. Armed with tape recorders duct-taped to their life vests, they spent half-days measuring, sexing and recording every short or over-sized lobster from every trap that came on deck. The first year, 78 lobstermen from Penobscot Bay harbors participated. (PC)

such patterns are correlated with known temperature readings from ships and buoys, it is possible to calibrate the reflected light data and assign sea surface temperature values.

In 1995 NESDIS launched a campaign to make sea surface temperature data as readily available—and usable—as satellite weather data. While sea surface data had been used by scientists studying the open ocean, much work remained to be done on the use of such data for coastal areas such as the Gulf of Maine and Penobscot Bay. NESDIS had recently launched several demonstration projects focused on coastal states' management problems, such as fisheries and toxic algae blooms.

Lee Dantzler, a NESDIS official, said his agency was "looking for a way to connect our investment in operational satellites with the practical information needs of citizens in different regions of the country."

"The request to help Maine address its questions about its coastal resources, especially its fisheries," Dantzler said, "fit nicely within our goal of increasing the amount of high quality satellite information for coastal users."

The Penobscot Bay Collaborative NESDIS agreed to make its archives more easily accessible to non-technical people such as fishermen, resource managers and educators. At the same time it would provide additional funding to scientists and resource agencies so they could use satellite data and other sources of information to build the capacity to understand the changing dynamics of complex marine environments.

Penobscot Bay was selected for research funding for a number of reasons. It is the largest bay on the coast of Maine and the second largest on the Atlantic coast of the United States, after Chesapeake Bay. The NESDIS funding was timely, as most ecological studies that had been conducted in the bay were environmental impact studies associated with development proposals for Sears Island, at the head of the bay. No set of comprehensive measurements had been taken to understand the basic ecology of the bay.

With NESDIS and the Island Institute, a group of state advisers began to plan a research program to link satellite data with practical questions about Penobscot Bay's changing marine environment. In a series of meetings that began in 1996, the advisers, NESDIS and the Institute developed the broad outlines for what became the Penobscot Bay Collaborative. From its early days the Collaborative's research and demonstration project agenda was guided by a State Advisory Committee consisting of (among others) representatives of Maine's Department of Marine Resources (DMR), Department of Environmental Protection (DEP) and the Coastal Program of the State Planning Office.

It was agreed at the outset that one long-term legacy of the effort should be an enhanced capacity to understand, access and utilize greater amounts of the nation's large investment in satellite technology, as well as information gained from other remotely sensed data. Finally, planners agreed that, to the maximum extent possible, all of the data collected from different sources would be

Dave Cousens

"YOUNG FISHERMEN HAVE ONLY SEEN GOOD TIMES."

The Penobscot Bay Collaborative has been well received by area fishermen because of its methodology, says Dave Cousens, president of the Maine Lobstermen's Association. It is essential to study the entire bay and its systems, he says, "in order to fully understand its complex nature."

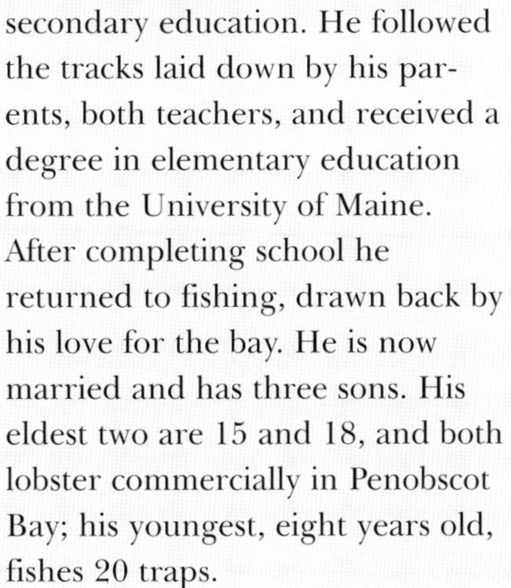
PETER RALSTON

The Collaborative has shown area lobstermen "how to look for indicators that offer insight into future landings and stock stability," he says. "It has also opened many fishermen's eyes as to what it takes to get lobsters on the bottom - younger fishermen have only seen good times, and we are fortunate that our management practices have been effective in sustaining substantial lobster stocks." He worries, however, that if the market or the lobsters were reduced, "many people would be out of business, and today so many more people lobster then a few decades ago, the bad times could be really bad."

Fishermen know that the best way to preserve Maine's lobster industry will be "a combination of research, observation, and conservation."

Born and raised in South Thomaston, Cousens has been lobstering in Penobscot Bay since he was nine years old. Despite his love of lobstering, he felt strongly that he wanted to pursue a post-secondary education. He followed the tracks laid down by his parents, both teachers, and received a degree in elementary education from the University of Maine. After completing school he returned to fishing, drawn back by his love for the bay. He is now married and has three sons. His eldest two are 15 and 18, and both lobster commercially in Penobscot Bay; his youngest, eight years old, fishes 20 traps.

(NN)

COURTESY MAINE MARITIME MUSEUM

Lobster labels from the nineteenth century when undersized lobsters were legally harvested, canned and shipped throughout the country.

reported in geographic terms and formatted into a Geographic Information System (GIS). The goal from the outset was to be able to compare different sets of information geographically.

Linda Mercer, the head of DMR's research division, recognized that in a complex region like Penobscot Bay, the NESDIS-funded Collaborative could potentially focus on many different questions and priorities.

There was an abundance of unanswered but related questions. Would Atlantic cod one day return to spawn in the bay? Where would nutrients from salmon aquaculture operations circulate through the bay? Why were clam harvests declining? The most pressing question, Mercer insisted, was to understand the patterns of distribution and abundance of Maine's valuable lobster resource. What was driving the increase in landings, and could the increase be sustained?

For many years, doubts had been growing about the techniques state and federal fisheries scientists were using to assess the status of lobsters in Maine and the Gulf of Maine. The National Marine Fisheries Service measures the abundance of lobsters by means of a bottom-trawl survey designed to catch fish, not lobsters, and doesn't operate in inshore waters because of potential conflicts with lobster gear. Maine's lobster sampling program, meanwhile, is limited in scope and therefore suspect in the minds of federal scientists. Harvests were going up, but could they be sustained? Or, as many feared, were lobsters being overfished?

Just as the Collaborative's effort to collect baseline ecological information throughout Penobscot Bay got underway, the Maine lobster population was officially designated as "overfished" by the National Marine Fisheries Service. The announcement infuriated most Maine lobstermen, whose experiences had been that lobsters— even juvenile lobsters—had never been more plentiful. Who was right? Mercer didn't know the answer; no one did. Therefore, the members of the Collaborative decided to focus, right away, on understanding the patterns of lobster distribution and abundance throughout Penobscot Bay.

Fishermen, historically skeptical of scientists and regulators, welcomed the Collaborative's efforts. Included in the process from the beginning, taking scientists on board to collect data and sharing their considerable knowledge of the bay, fishermen trusted that the Collaborative's efforts would help to tell the real story behind the bay's expanding lobster fishery.

NICK CALOYIANIS

PETER RALSTON

2

Currents and Gyres

WHAT GOES AROUND COMES AROUND

THE COLLABORATIVE'S FIRST STEP toward understanding the lobster population was to understand Penobscot Bay's ecosystem, beginning with its dominant feature: circulation.

From the top of Mount Battie above Camden, the view on a clear day includes nearly all of Penobscot Bay. It is natural enough, therefore, to think of the bay as a place with distinct geographic and ecological boundaries. Efforts to understand it and manage its single most valuable resource, its lobster fishery, have also been scaled to its geography. But important factors affecting the bay's circulation operate at a much a larger scale than is apparent at first.

Most of us probably assume that the waters of the bay, flushed by twice daily tides, are fairly uniform from top to bottom and from one end to the other. But the waters here have a structure that is surprisingly distinct and persistent. Because the bay's currents affect their boats, gear and catches, Penobscot Bay's fishermen know well that the waters of the bay differ from place to place, from surface to bottom and from season to season. For example, traps set in the mouth of the western bay require extra line and larger buoys because the currents flow one direction on the surface and the opposite direction at depth, putting tremendous strain on the lines. Fishermen are well aware that hauling these traps is harder work due to the lack of slack in the line. In Carver's Harbor, on Vinalhaven, surface currents flow in one direction and less than a mile away flow in the opposite direction. Seasoned fishermen know just when to reverse their approach to buoys in order to come up on them into the current. From the top of Mount Battie, even the casual observer will note the point at which spring runoff from the Penobscot River, brown from its load of silt, mixes mid-bay with blue-green ocean water.

Until the Penobscot Bay Collaborative began its work, most everyone believed that the bay was a typical estuary dominated by the influence of the Penobscot River's fresh water surge at the head of the bay. There were only vague ideas of how offshore oceanographic currents moved affected the rest of the bay. Ultimately most of the initial ideas about the bay's currents were proved wrong.

An initial goal of the Penobscot Bay Collaborative was to describe the structure of the bay's water masses which differ not only in temperature and salinity, but also in speed and direction. Currents are critical to understanding the bay's ecosystem; through transport and mixing processes they strongly affect the biology of the bay. An ecosystem is often described as the interaction of physical factors such as weather events and seasonal shifts in temperature, and biological factors such as competition and predation. In some ecosystems (for example, rain forests) biological factors predominate. In Penobscot Bay as in many marine systems, physical factors (in this case, the dynamics of circulation) are the crucial factors driving the system.

Neal Pettigrew, a physical oceanographer at the University of Maine, designed and conducted a research program to characterize Penobscot Bay's currents further. Pettigrew's earlier work in the Gulf of Maine had added important new information to our understanding of patterns of circulation, patterns first described by Henry Bigelow in the 1920s. Where Bigelow used a sailing vessel to collect water samples and set out drift bottles, Pettigrew relied on oceanographic research vessels equipped with electronic instruments to measure temperature and salinity. Using sophisticated oceanographic buoys with current meters, temperature and salinity sensors and satellite-tracked surface drifters, he constructed a circulation picture.

Bigelow had discovered that the waters of the Gulf of Maine are comprised of large, circular flows, known as "gyres": one counterclockwise, encompassing the interior of the Gulf of Maine, and a second clockwise around Georges Bank. Later work by David Brooks, a physical oceanographer at Texas A&M University, and others, in the 1980s, showed that the counterclockwise circulation of the Gulf of Maine consisted of a gyre in the eastern gulf centered over the Jordan Basin, and a somewhat weaker counterclockwise circulation in the western gulf.

Pettigrew confirmed the existence of these gyres. In addition, he discovered another gyre in the eastern Gulf of Maine centered over Georges Basin. Thus the circulation pattern in the eastern Gulf could be characterized as a coupled pair of gyres each flowing counterclockwise. The combination of these gyres could allow waters from downeast Maine to reach Georges Bank in approximately a month, by steering them offshore near Penobscot Bay.

A New Picture Pettigrew had obtained the first long-term direct measurements of the Eastern Maine Coastal Current, which flows southwesterly from Grand Manan Island in New Brunswick to the mouth of Penobscot Bay, and had described its general nature. However, how this large-scale oceanographic current interacted with any of the coastal embayments along its route remained unexplored. Whether, when and how the Eastern Maine Coastal Current interacts with Penobscot Bay became a central question for the Penobscot Bay Collaborative, and

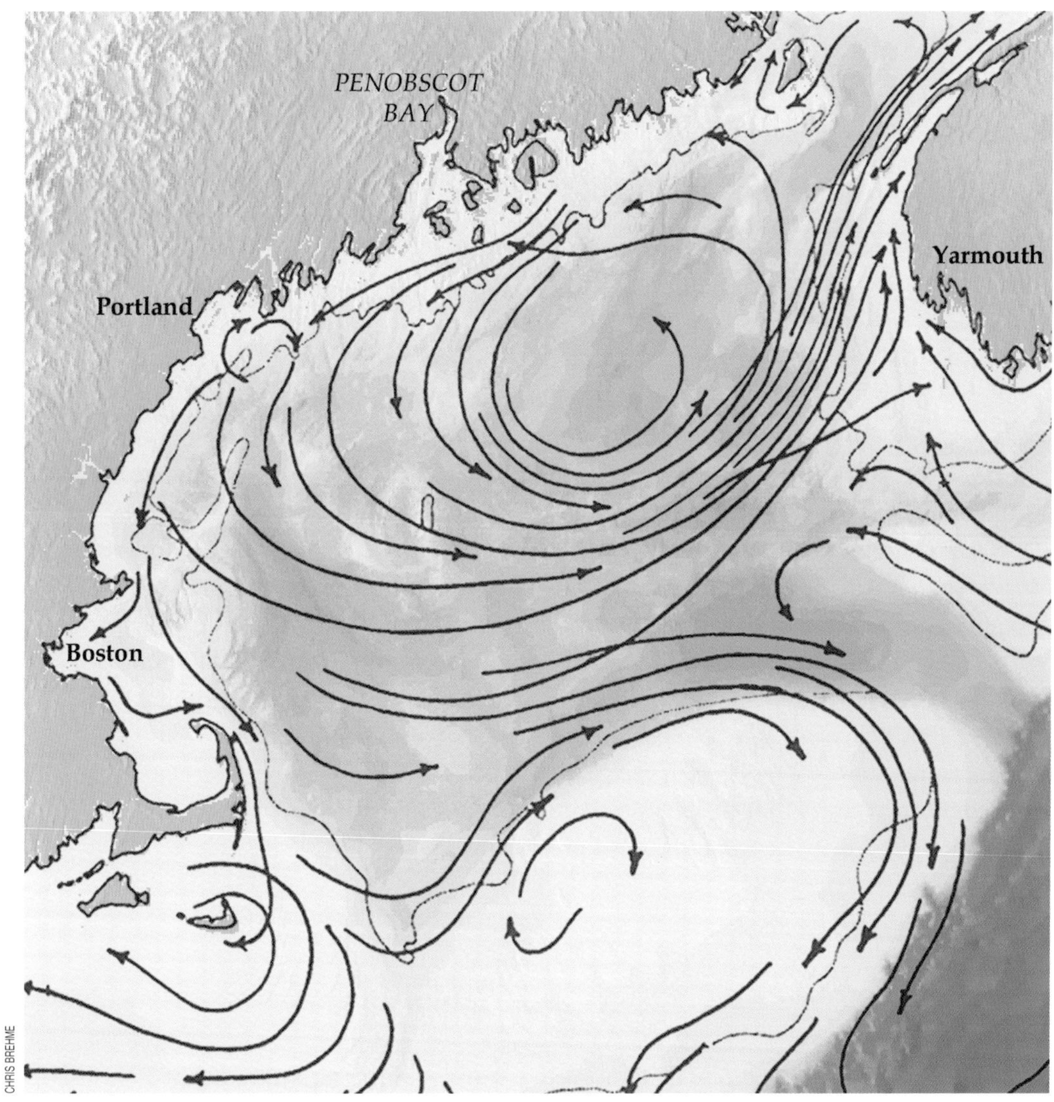

CHRIS BREHME

In 1928, after years of launching and following drift bottles in the Gulf of Maine, Henry Bigelow published the first map of the Gulf's major circulation features. Bigelow's stunning accomplishment, which defined two large gyres over Georges Bank and around the rim of the Gulf, was not revised for another 70 years.

became crucial to understanding the circulation and the ecosystem of Penobscot Bay.

Nearshore waters like those of Penobscot Bay present challenges in conducting oceanographic research: landforms, bathymetry and land-based weather patterns affect currents in complex ways. Oceanographers have tended to study offshore waters (where currents have larger spatial scales) to try to understand the dynamics of oceanic circulation. Nearshore waters are relatively poorly understood, even though they are extremely productive and support the vast majority of human maritime activity. At the outset of the Collaborative's efforts, it was clear that basic oceanographic information about the nearshore waters would be critical to understanding them. Such understanding, in turn, would be vital to their

Neal Pettigrew
SORTING OUT THE COMPLEXITY

DAVID TOWNSEND, UNIVERSITY OF MAINE

Neal Pettigrew, Ph.D., an Associate Professor of Oceanography at the University of Maine, specializes in the study of coastal circulation processes. He has conducted experiments on the east, west and Gulf coasts of the United States, as well as in more remote locales including the Strait of Gibraltar and the South China Sea. In these studies he employs state-of-the-art oceanographic technology, including automated solar-powered data buoys developed in his research laboratory. In analyzing the resulting data, Pettigrew employs a broad array of statistical analyses and the techniques of theoretical fluid dynamics.

During the past decade he has broadened his research effort to include the links between circulation processes and the biological components of the ecosystem such as the initiation of algal blooms and "red tides," larval distributions and the environmental impact of finfish aquaculture. As chief scientist for the Gulf of Maine Ocean Observing System (GoMOOS), he has recently deployed an extensive system of buoys in the gulf as part of a real-time monitoring system that delivers a suite of oceanographic observations to the World Wide Web.

"The Gulf of Maine marine ecosystem is fascinating in its complexity and in its relationship to the system of fluid mechanics that support it," Pettigrew says. "Perhaps nowhere in the United States is the relationship between fish and physics more evident."

(AH)

effective management.

Before the Penobscot Bay Collaborative, most scientists assumed that Penobscot Bay was a typical estuary —that its circulation pattern was dominated by fresh water entering the bay from the Penobscot River riding up over a "wedge" of denser (and therefore heavier) salt water coming in from the Gulf of Maine. However, surface temperature patterns observed from satellites led them to suspect that the cold waters of the Eastern Maine Coastal Current might be entering Penobscot Bay. To test this hypothesis, Pettigrew placed monitoring buoys in the two main channels of east and west Penobscot Bay. The sensors mounted on the buoys collected data around the clock, for months at a time, on current direction and speed, water temperature and salinity.

Initially Pettigrew retrieved his data from the buoys when they were brought in

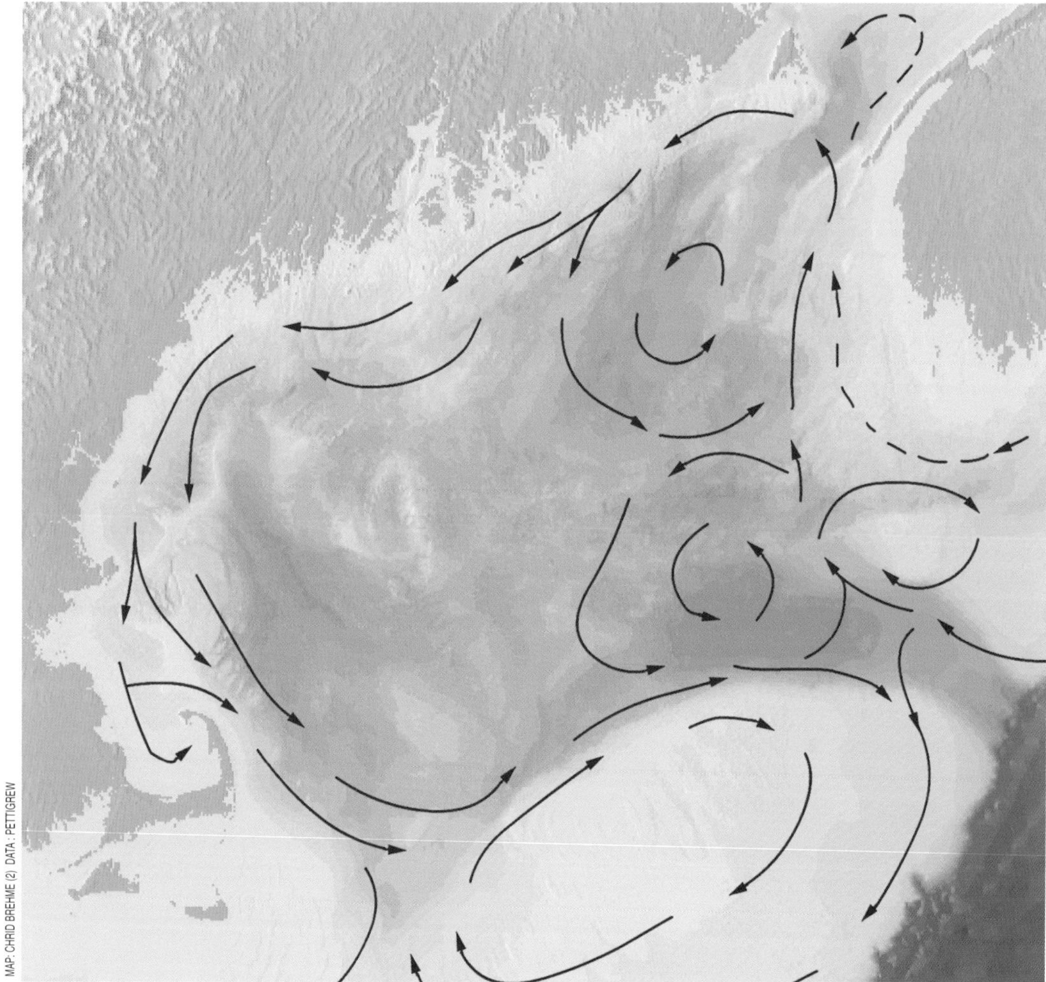

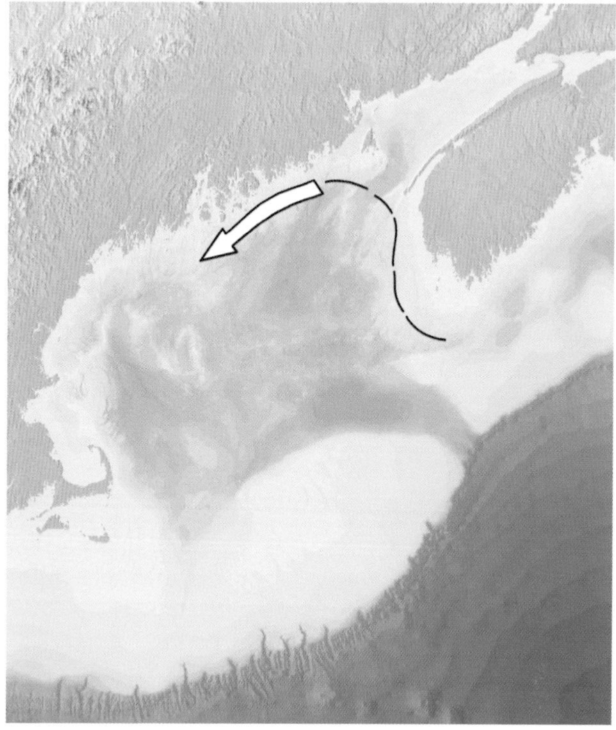

Left: In 1998, Neil Pettigrew published a map of the circulation of the Gulf of Maine that described additional gyres in the eastern Gulf of Maine.
Above: Eastern Maine Coastal Current is the major circulation feature of the Maine coast between Canada and Penobscot Bay.

at the end of a season. Then he rigged his buoys with cellular phones programmed to transmit the computerized data back to his lab daily - an innovative application of an established technology that allowed him ready access to the data and to know immediately when a sensor had stopped functioning or if a buoy was adrift.

To provide additional spatial data and to ensure that the buoys were placed appropriately, Pettigrew also conducted several hydrographic cruises in the bay and and conferred with Deirdre Byrne, a physical oceanographer working first with the Island Institute and then with the University of Maine. Byrne had analyzed satellite images of the bay, data on river flow measured at Eddington on the Penobscot River, and temperature and salinity data collected by students at the Maine Maritime Academy. She observed that the effect of river flow appeared to be limited to the northwestern part of the bay, and that conversely, waters east of

Vinalhaven were most similar to the oceanic waters of the Gulf of Maine. This context established that the hydrographic conditions observed in the first year of the Penobscot Bay Collaborative were typical conditions for this region.

On his hydrographic cruises Pettigrew collected data on current speed and direction, water temperature and salinity at stations throughout the bay. These data were collected repeatedly over a tidal cycle, allowing him to subtract the effect of the tides and reveal underlying current direction and speed.

Pettigrew's analysis yielded surprising results. Instead of confirming that the bay's primary circulation pattern is estuarine in character, he found that Penobscot

Deploying one a of a new generation of oceanographic buoys with cell phones mounted on top that are programmed to 'phone home' data that can be collected and analyzed without having to retrieve the buoy.

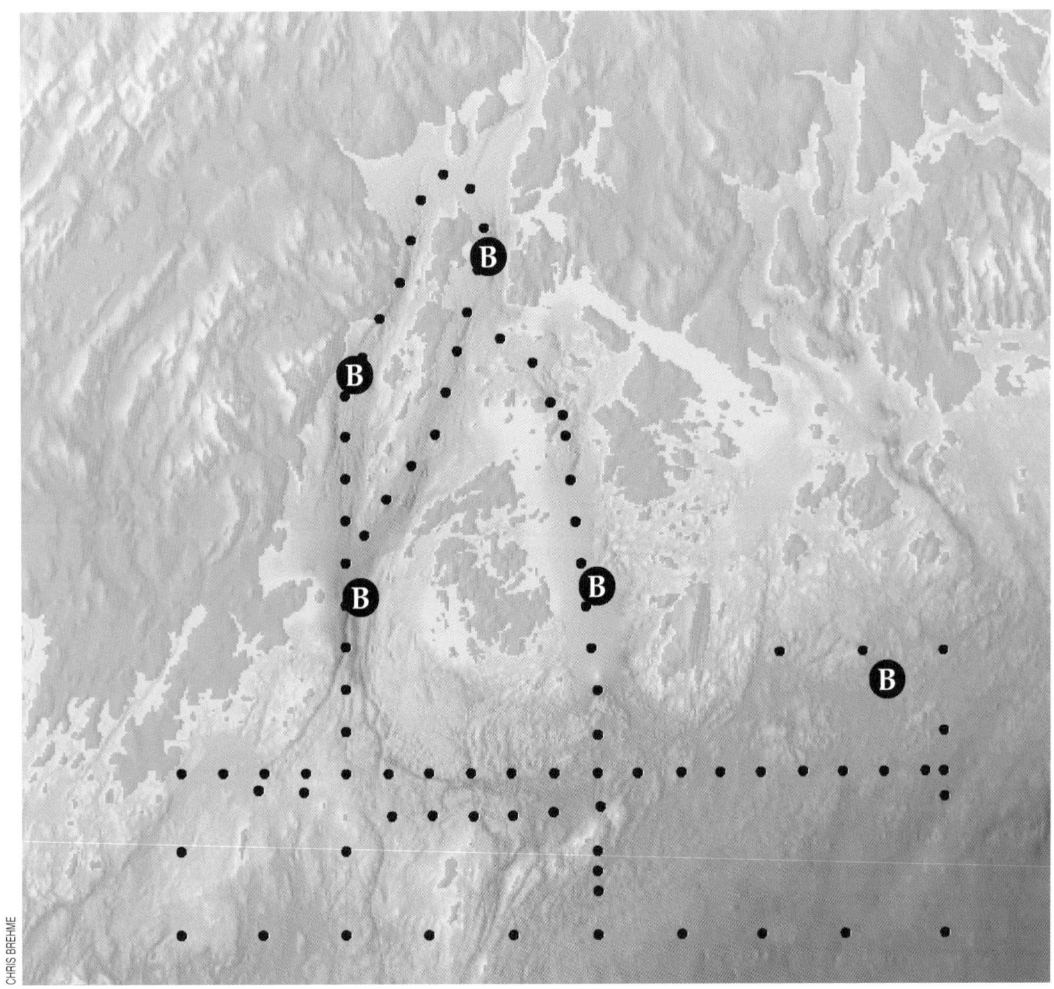

The location of Pettigrew's buoy array (B) and the hydrographic stations where he collected measurements.

Bay is in fact dominated by exchange with the Gulf of Maine to the south. Strong net inflow occurred on the western side of the bay, balanced by outflow observed to the east of Vinalhaven. Remarkably, the inflow found its strongest near-surface expression during the spring and summer months when runoff from the river is at its peak. An important early finding, therefore, is that Penobscot Bay is primarily a marine system dominated by full strength seawater. The influence of fresh water input from the Penobscot River's massive watershed pales in comparison to the strength of the ocean currents entering the outer bay.

To explain the dramatic and unexpected inflow of seawater, Pettigrew theorized that a portion of the Eastern Maine Coastal Current branches off and heads north, into the bay, while the main body of the current heads south towards Georges Bank, or at times, continues westward along the shelf.

Drifting for Details Having determined that inflow to the bay from the Eastern Maine Coastal Current was significant, Pettigrew began to analyze the details of this flow. The predominant flow of water, he found, was into the western bay, between Vinalhaven and Rockland. It was compensated by outflow from the eastern bay, creating gyres, or circular flows, around the large, mid-bay islands of Islesboro, North Haven and Vinalhaven.

To confirm the buoy data, Pettigrew also conducted drifter studies to provide an additional test of his hypothesis that the island gyres represented the mean pathway of the inflowing seawater. The four drifters consisted of 20-foot fabric tubes attached to buoys at the surface that act like underwater "wind socks." Deployed on 45-foot lines to move with the currents at depth, each buoy contained a signaling device and was tracked by a communications satellite. The satellite recorded the position of Pettigrew's drifters several times a day and forwarded the information daily to his lab. Reading the output, Pettigrew could follow the track of the drifters and determine if they had stopped moving, needed to be freed from lobster gear or a sand bar, or had circumnavigated the mid-bay islands and needed to be retrieved before heading out to sea.

Released in the channel between Rockland and Vinalhaven, the drifters were tracked for the several weeks it took them to make significant headway. Despite entanglements with fishing gear and one or two well-intended retrievals by fishermen who took them ashore, these instruments clearly demarcated the existence of

PETER RALSTON

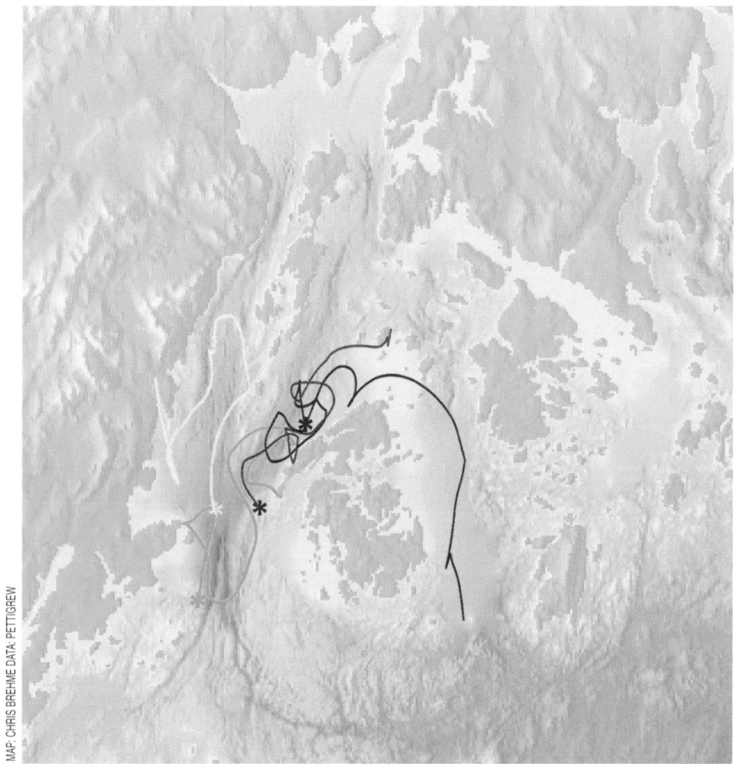

MAP: CHRIS BREHME DATA: PETTIGREW

Pettigrew's drifter experiments during the summer of 2000 (left) and 2001 (right) clearly confirmed the clockwise circular gyres around the mid-bay islands of Vinalhaven and North Haven. The yellow drifter line from the 2000 experiment was found by the Rockport Harbormaster and brought ashore.

the mid-bay gyre. Pettigrew had confirmed that subsurface currents in the west bay travel northward from the outer part of the Gulf of Maine and circle around the large, mid-bay islands.

An Oceanic System The currents in and out of the bay are not uniform from the surface to bottom. In summer, while most of the water in the west bay is flowing north, the surface layer and bottom layer are flowing south. The three dimensional circulation pattern can be thought of as two counter rotating gyres, stacked one on another, with the thin layer of outward-flowing river water laid on top. The major feature is the clockwise gyre in which water enters the bay west of Vinalhaven and exits on the east. Near the bottom a smaller counterclockwise gyre brings the densest waters into the bay east of Vinalhaven and expels it from the deep channel on the western side of the Islands. Pettigrew has identified a seasonal transition where, from mid-September until April, surface outflows in the western bay deepen; currents flowing in at depth become stronger. This deepening is not due to increased flow from the Penobscot River, since September brings the lowest river flows of the year. It is probably related to major changes in the flow, and possibly position, of the Eastern Maine Coastal Current.

The 3-layered structure of circulation features in the water column of Penobscot Bay (above). Major circulation patterns in Penobscot Bay based on four seasons of Pettigrew's measurements (facing page).

Currents in the western bay are more distinctly layered than they are in the east bay. This may be due, Pettigrew thinks, to the mixing effect of the archipelago of small islands to the northeast of North Haven. As water flowing from west to east around the top of North Haven encounters these islands, as well as underwater shoals, its layers are broken up and combined.

The upper bay near Islesboro is more estuarine than the lower bay. Here, the Penobscot River flows out over incoming currents from the ocean. However, even in the upper bay, currents originating from the Gulf of Maine play a significant role.

Pettigrew's work shows that Penobscot Bay is not a distinct entity that can be understood by analyzing only the waters within its borders. The currents of the Gulf of Maine - the Eastern Maine Coastal Current in particular - are integral to the life of the bay. But what drives the Gulf's currents? Oceanographers have described inputs to the Gulf of Maine from the Scotian Shelf, an area to the south and east of Nova Scotia. These flows are part of a much larger cycle of flows in the North Atlantic. These flows, in turn, are part of a complex interaction with the atmosphere. These complex linkages remind us that we must be aware of the larger systems to which Penobscot Bay is connected if we are to understand its ecosystem fully. In ecology, everything is connected to everything else.

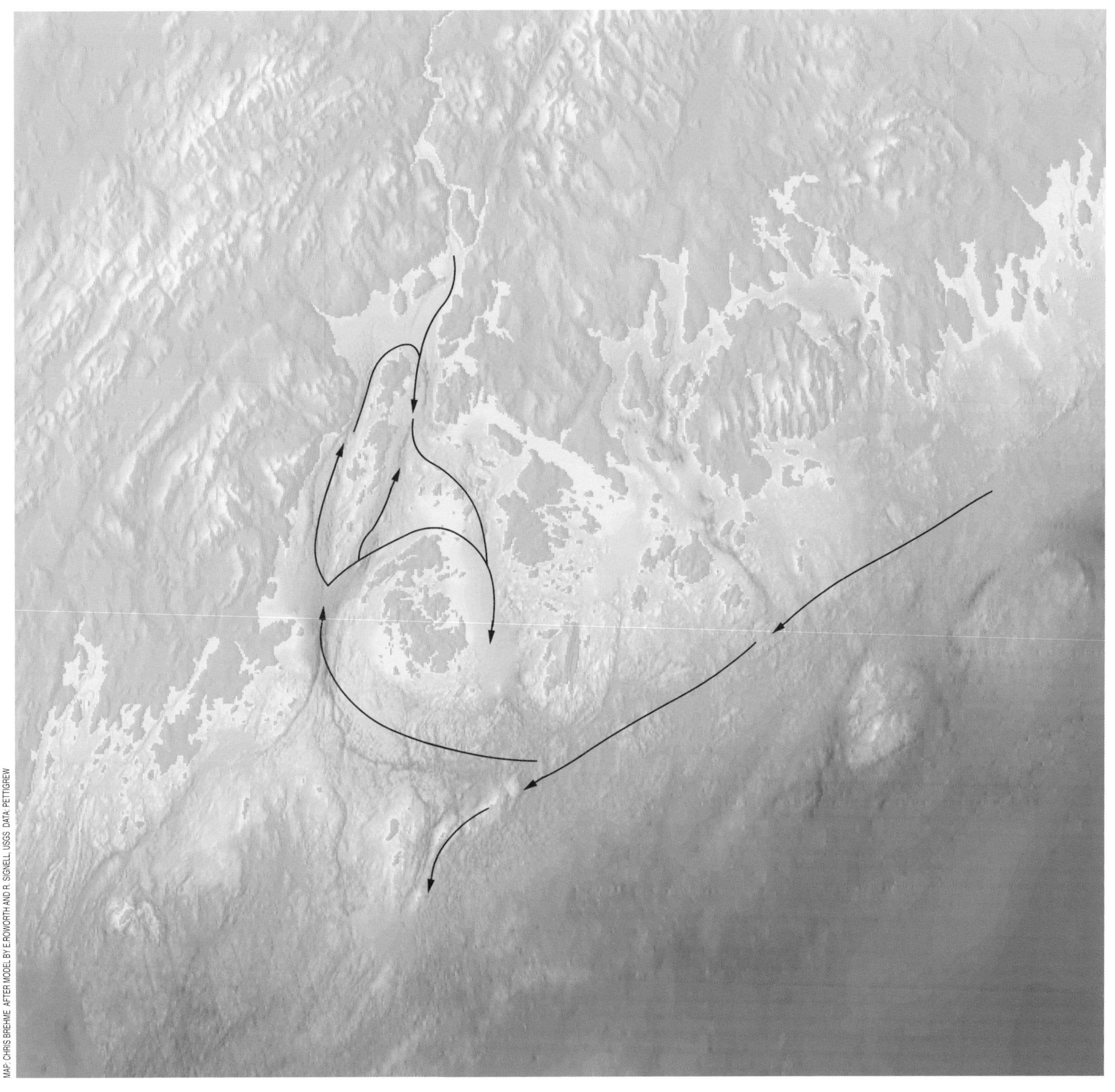

MAP: CHRIS BREHME AFTER MODEL BY E.ROWORTH AND R. SIGNELL, USGS DATA: PETTIGREW

PETER RALSTON

3

Getting the Big Picture

THE VIEW FROM SPACE

TO EXPAND THE UNDERSTANDING OF PENOBSCOT BAY'S ecosystem and the bay's link to larger ecosystems, the Collaborative took advantage of several relatively new tools. Loosely grouped under the term "remote sensing," these tools make use of sensors deployed on airplanes, boats and satellites, and are designed to measure a variety of oceanographic parameters from water temperature and color to sediment type at a variety of scales.

The study of the oceans has for decades involved the collection of "field" data - working from a research vessel, measuring temperature, salinity and currents; collecting water samples to determine its chemistry, and plankton samples to analyze microscopic plant and animal life. But one can sample in only one place at a time and collect a limited number of samples. Furthermore, the expense of chartering a research vessel can be prohibitive.

Automated data collectors, deployed on buoys, have helped overcome such limitations. Such buoys can provide data from several points simultaneously, often continuously for the period of deployment. Remote sensing provides yet another expansion of the oceanographer's ability to understand processes at work in the Gulf of Maine and Penobscot Bay; both in space (how water masses differ from one shore of the bay to the other, from the bottom to the surface) but also in time: changes with tides and seasons.Remote sensing devices have provided the oceanographer with further information to test his or her vision of what's happening in the water.

Satellite imagery provides essential large-scale regional pictures of changing daily, weekly and seasonal temperature patterns across the entire Gulf of Maine with close up views of Penobscot Bay. Permanent temperature 'fronts,' discovered during the course of the Collaborative's work, between warmer and colder water masses, have important biological consequences for many marine species, especially lobsters.

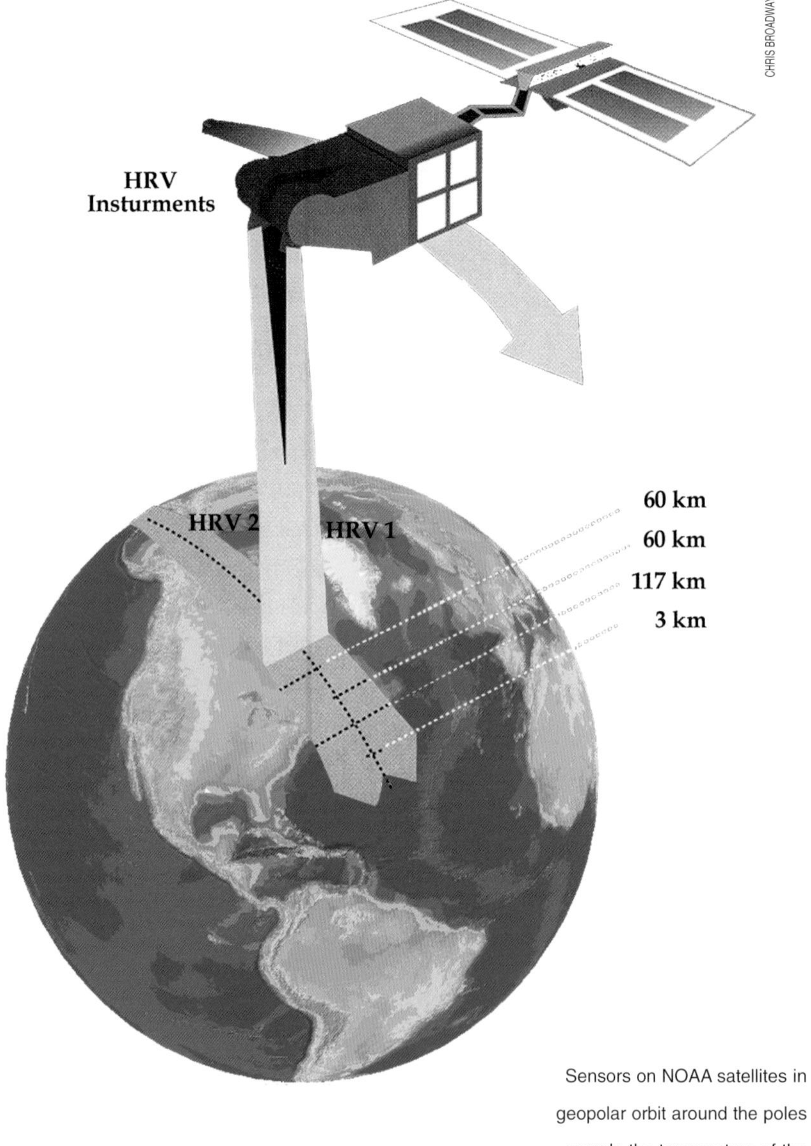

Sensors on NOAA satellites in geopolar orbit around the poles sample the temperature of the surface of ocean waters in large swaths as they travel from pole to pole while the earth spins underneath to provide world wide coverage

Scale Can Be Critical Joe Kelley, a geologist working at the University of Maine, used sidescan sonar to analyze the sediments of Penobscot Bay. Towing an instrument behind his research vessel, Kelley was able to map the distribution of cobble bottom, the preferred habitat of juvenile lobsters. Mark Lazarri, a scientist with the Maine Department of Marine Resources, made use of a similar instrument to analyze the habitat preferences of groundfish. A sophisticated visual sensor, taking multi-spectral measurements through a hole in the bottom of an airplane, collected very detailed information on the characteristics of intertidal habitats that could be used by Peter Larsen and Cyndy Erickson of the Bigelow Laboratory to develop a classification of intertidal habitats.

Orbiting miles above the Earth, instruments on satellites are the most "remote" of the new tools, and often they generate a great deal of data. Developed initially by the military to gather intelligence, satellite data have come to play an important role in gathering information about our natural resources and the environment. They are essential to routine weather prediction and are vital in predicting the potential impacts of hurricanes, floods and forest fires.

The immense volume of information becomes an issue when using remotely sensed data. The images of intertidal habitat acquired for the Collaborative, for example, are high resolution, made up of a grid of small rectangles called "pixels" that capture information on habitat, from an area only four meters on each side. The effort required to acquire and process such dense data means it is limited to relatively small areas. Intertidal habitat data collected in Penobscot Bay was limited to two test areas, one around Islesboro, the other in the Weskeag River.

Ocean temperature information collected by an Advanced Very High Resolution Radiometer (AVHRR) on board a satellite, in contrast, has a pixel size of 1.1 kilometers squared. At this resolution, temperature information for the bay is fairly crude; however, this satellite sensor is an excellent tool for capturing the pattern of surface temperature within the much larger Gulf of Maine.

Scale is important not only in terms of the size of the area imaged but also in terms of the time lapse between images. Aerial reconnaissance of the two intertidal habitat sites was conducted just once; it is very expensive to collect a second set of data for assessing changes over time. Again, in contrast, the AVHRR-bearing satellites pass over the Gulf of Maine four to six times a day. Trends from day to day, season to season and year to year can be compared and contrasted, and the temporal longevity of ocean patterns can be assessed.

Choosing among remotely sensed data products frequently involves making tradeoffs among frequency of image production, the level of detail in the data and the size of the area that can be analyzed.

The capacity of satellites to collect images of Penobscot Bay and the Gulf of Maine from space is astonishing, but it is only the beginning. The data, which are generated in huge amounts day in and day out throughout the year, must be carefully processed on very powerful computers in order to yield meaningful information.

Satellite-derived temperature data used in the Penobscot Bay Project must be processed through a series of steps to ensure its accuracy. The effect on the satellite signal of passing through the atmosphere must be taken into account and areas masked by clouds must be adjusted or deleted.

Creating a Baseline Using data on sea surface temperature, Andrew Thomas of the University of Maine has compiled a series of long-term averages called "climatologies" that are used to assess trends.

Seasonal analysis of the Gulf of Maine, for example, shows that in the winter, the coldest water is near shore with warmer water offshore; in the summer, this pattern is reversed. Thomas's climatologies now include 13 years' worth of satellite data. Such long-term averages can be compared to data from individual years to assess the variation in surface temperature. Comparison of such data to biological measurements allow oceanographers to assess the role of ocean temperature in the Gulf of Maine ecosystem.

One advantage of AVHRR data is the geographic range or coverage; oceanographers can test the significance of surface temperature variability at a range of

PETER RALSTON

scales. Thomas has noted, for example, that variations from the annual average temperature within Penobscot Bay are matched by similar variations in the Eastern Maine Coastal Current.

By comparing variations in surface temperature with variations in biological data, such as changes in the abundance of fish stocks or the productivity of plant life, scientists add to their understanding of the relative importance of oceanographic factors in the functioning of the ecosystem. They also learn more about the scale of such effects.

Currently, Thomas is comparing long-term temperature trends with levels of lobster larval settlement. The results may indicate a relationship between the two. While temperature affects the rate of growth of lobster larvae (and therefore their readiness to settle), the more important role of satellite data here is to indicate the presence and location of currents. The Eastern Maine Coastal Current, for example, may play a role in the delivery and retention of larvae within Penobscot Bay.

Making the Connections Satellites can only "see" the surface of the ocean. One goal of the Penobscot Bay research team has been to understand the relationship between surface temperature data measured by satellites, and information collected below the surface by research vessels and automated data collectors. On a daily basis, differences often appear between satellite and field data. But when the two were combined to reflect a season's or a year's worth of measurements, Thomas found, the satellite data were consistent with information on subsurface currents collected by Pettigrew. Both field and satellite data revealed the existence of fronts or temperature shifts off Owls Head near the mouth of the bay and outside of the bay off Port Clyde. Both showed that the west bay is warmer in summer and colder in winter than the east bay. In addition, satellite analysis showed that the Eastern Maine Coastal Current is consistently visible from week to week over the summer and fall; it is a notably stable oceanographic feature in the Gulf of Maine.

Deirdre Byrne, an oceanographer at the Island Institute and subsequently at the University of Maine, and Thomas combined the benefits of calibrated AVHRR surface temperature data with the greater detail of another type of satellite data, called Landsat. As the name implies, Landsat data are intended to capture environmental data from terrestrial environments. Its temperature data boasts a spatial resolution of 120 meters squared. The satellite's temperature sensor works as well on water as land but, uncalibrated and not atmospherically corrected, it generates only a relative scale of sea surface temperatures.

Using 23 Landsat images taken from 1986 to 1996, Byrne and Thomas matched each image with an AVHRR image from the same date. Byrne and

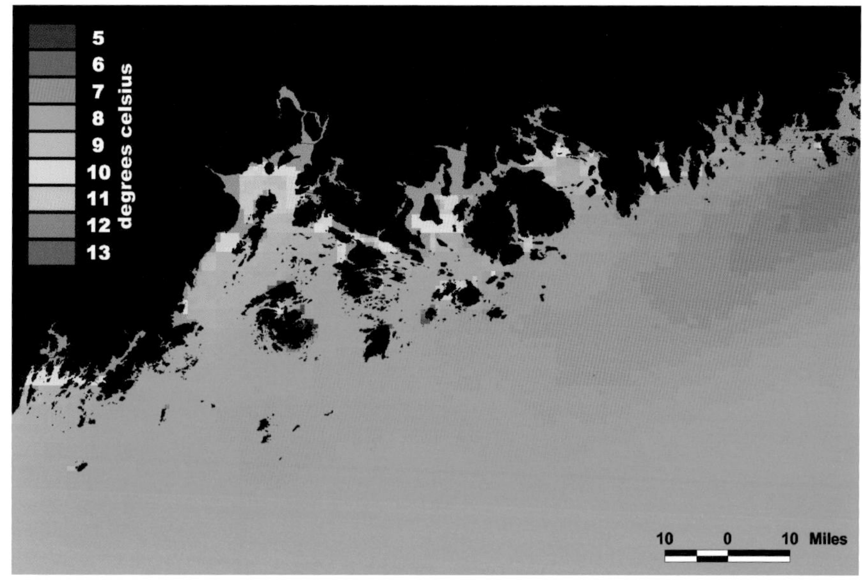

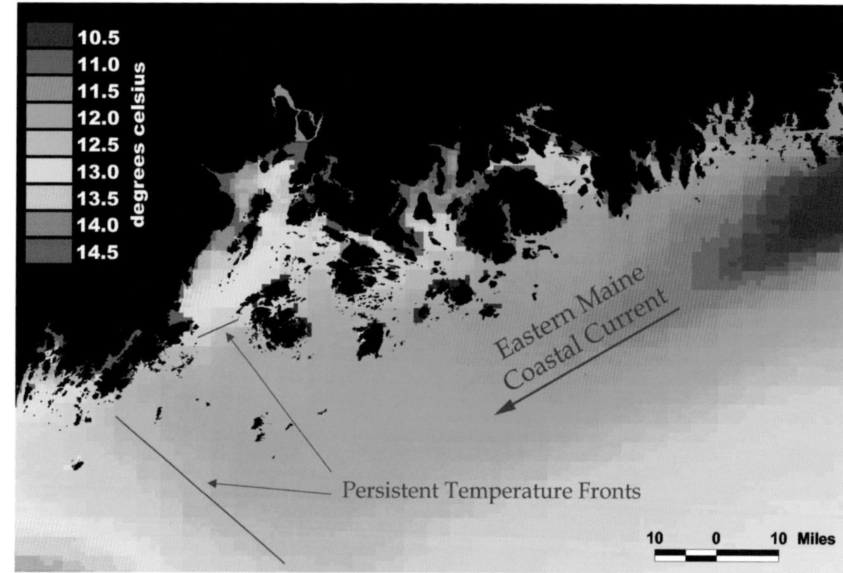

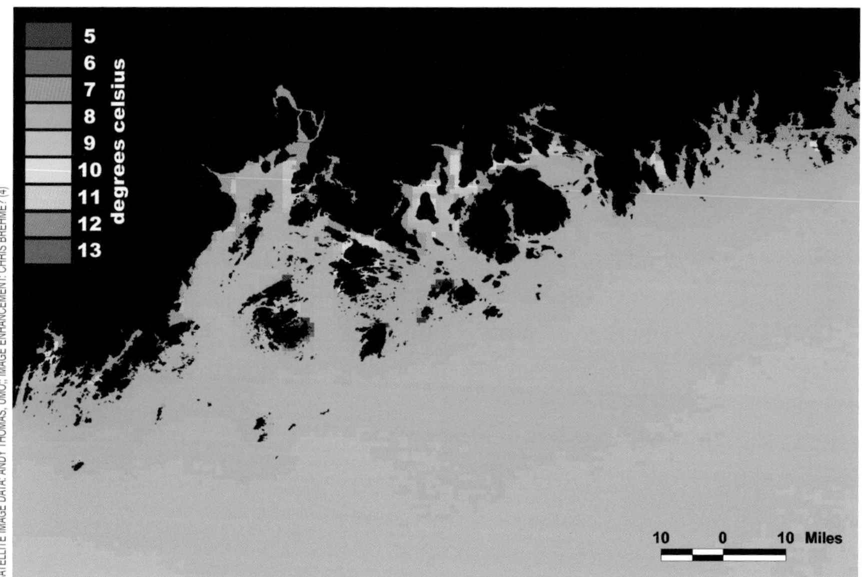

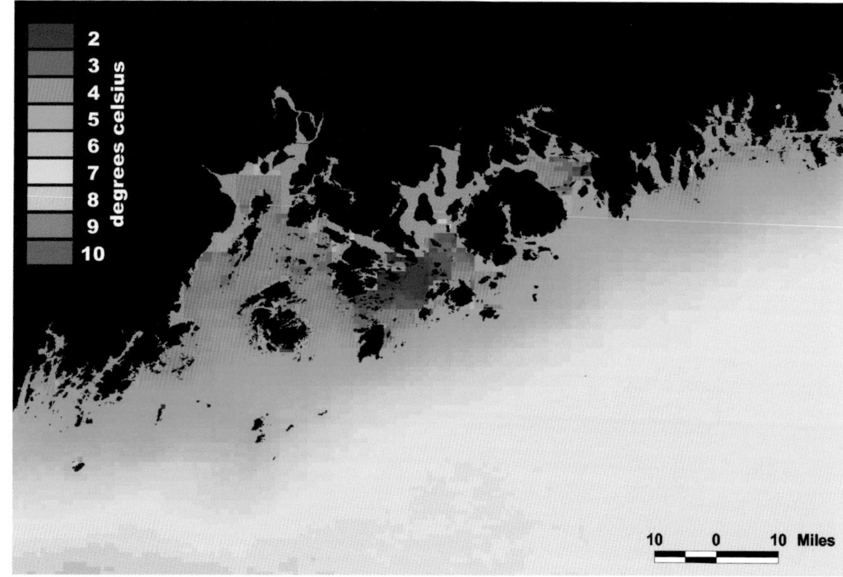

SATELLITE IMAGE DATA: ANDY THOMAS, UMO;; IMAGE ENHANCEMENT: CHRIS BREHME? (4)

13 year seasonal sea surface temperature averages 1987-1999. Clockwise from top left: spring (April-June), showing the presence of the Eastern Maine Coastal Current; summer, (July-Sept) showing the formation of the persistent temperature fronts in surface waters of western Penobscot Bay; fall (Oct-Dec), showing the uniformity of sea surfaces temperatures throughout the eastern Gulf of Maine; winter (Jan-Mar), showing the warmer waters offshore and the cold waters up in the bays near land.

PETER RALSTON

View of the Eastern Maine Coastal Current from sea level off Cape Split, Addison

SHAPING THE DATA

Infrared satellite data measure the thermal properties of the ocean surface, but need to be corrected for the intervening influence of the atmosphere. Without this correction, the data measure only relative patterns of surface temperature.

The NASA/NOAA Pathfinder Project at the University of Miami takes the process one step further. It compares the results of many years of satellite sea surface temperature with global field data collected by buoys, research vessels and commercial ships as they travel from port to port. The field data is compared with the satellite results for the date and place of the field sample to assess the rigor of the image processing analysis.

Peter Cornillon, at the University of Rhode Island, duplicates this process to create a high resolution product for the eastern seaboard of the United States. When the process, which can take over two years, is complete, the final product is forwarded electronically to the Satellite Oceanographic Data Laboratory at the University of Maine, run by Andrew Thomas.

Thomas further refines the data by creating subsets and research products that focus on Penobscot Bay and the Eastern Maine Coastal Current. One important early correction to the Rhode Island processing he made was an adjustment to the image area masked out as cloudy. With this adjustment, coastal areas, including much of Penobscot Bay were retained and made available for analysis.

Over 13 years' worth of data, each with three to five images per day, have been analyzed, making for a large data set - over 19,000 images occupying over 20 gigabytes. These provide detailed spatial maps for each month, showing which years had relatively warm surface temperatures and which years had cold temperatures. Importantly, these maps show the relationship between different locations of these interannual differences. For example, if the Owl's Head region showed much warmer surface temperatures in the spring of a particular year, did other regions have similar anomalies, or was it completely local.. These data are now being compared to factors such as differences in wind strength and currents, allowing managers to investigate linkages between resource fluctuations and ocean features over the past 13 years. (AH)

PETER RALSTON

Thomas used the calibrated AVHRR temperature data to assign values to the relative scale of temperature in the Landsat images.

The results allowed for a more detailed analysis of the spatial pattern of surface temperature in Penobscot Bay. At this greater level of detail, satellite data were again consistent with field measurements of oceanographic conditions within the bay. The color of the ocean is monitored by the satellite-borne Sea-viewing Wide-Field-of-view Sensor (SeaWiFS) and is used to estimate chlorophyll levels and phytoplankton biomass in the ocean. Formulas to interpret such data are still under development, and nearshore waters such as Penobscot Bay present particular difficulties, since water-borne sediments and organic matter can interfere with the signal generated by chlorophyll. As a result, estimates of plant growth can be exaggerated. Satellite data are collected on a regular and ongoing basis and are available on a nearly instantaneous, or real-time, basis. Downloading the most recent cloud-free images of their study area to onboard computers, researchers can fine-tune their sampling programs to target particular water masses and currents. For example, satellite data can be helpful in identifying areas where different water bodies meet, called frontal zones, which are of special interest to scientists because they tend to be rich in marine plant and animal life.

Andrew Thomas

PROVIDING CRITICAL CONTEXT

Andrew Thomas, an oceanographer at the University of Maine, focuses on extracting information from the billions of bits of satellite data that his lab receives each week. Thomas's research is centered on finding, quantifying and explaining patterns in time and space that the satellite data see in the ocean. An ongoing project is an analysis of surface temperature and ocean color variability in the Gulf of Maine on seasonal and longer time scales. Because averages, or climatologies, describe an important source of variability in the Gulf of Maine ecosystem, they provide critical context for much of the marine research and management efforts underway both in the gulf and in Penobscot Bay.

NAKOMIS NELSON

A great deal of decidedly unglamorous number crunching is required to make sense of the torrent of data flowing into Thomas's computers at the School of Marine Sciences. The resulting information products, on the other hand, are elegant and reflect his thoughtful design and analysis. Converted into GIS layers, the information is displayed as rainbow-hued maps. Warmer waters are portrayed with tints from the warm end of the color spectrum and cooler waters vice versa. The resulting graphics are intuitively clear; the cooler waters of the Bay of Fundy, the Eastern Maine Coastal Current and Georges Bank are readily apparent.

Products that compare these climatologies with data from each individual year highlight, for the first time, the magnitude and spatial patterns of interannual variability in the Gulf of Maine. Thomas has put the climatology into a video clip that represents the long-term average annual cycle of surface temperature over the Gulf. The differing amplitude of the annual cycle at each location and mid-winter mixing that occurs when the cooling of the surface layer causes it to sink, are visible. The reversal of inshore-offshore temperature gradients is also clear: inshore waters are warm in the summer and cool in the winter; offshore waters are buffered by mixing with deeper waters - relative to inshore waters, they are warmer in the winter and cooler in the summer.

"Satellite data are another important tool oceanographers use in understanding the dynamics of marine ecosystems," Thomas says. "These data complement field and numerical model data in a way that makes all three much more valuable."

(BN)

IMAGE ENHANCEMENT: CHRIS BREHME

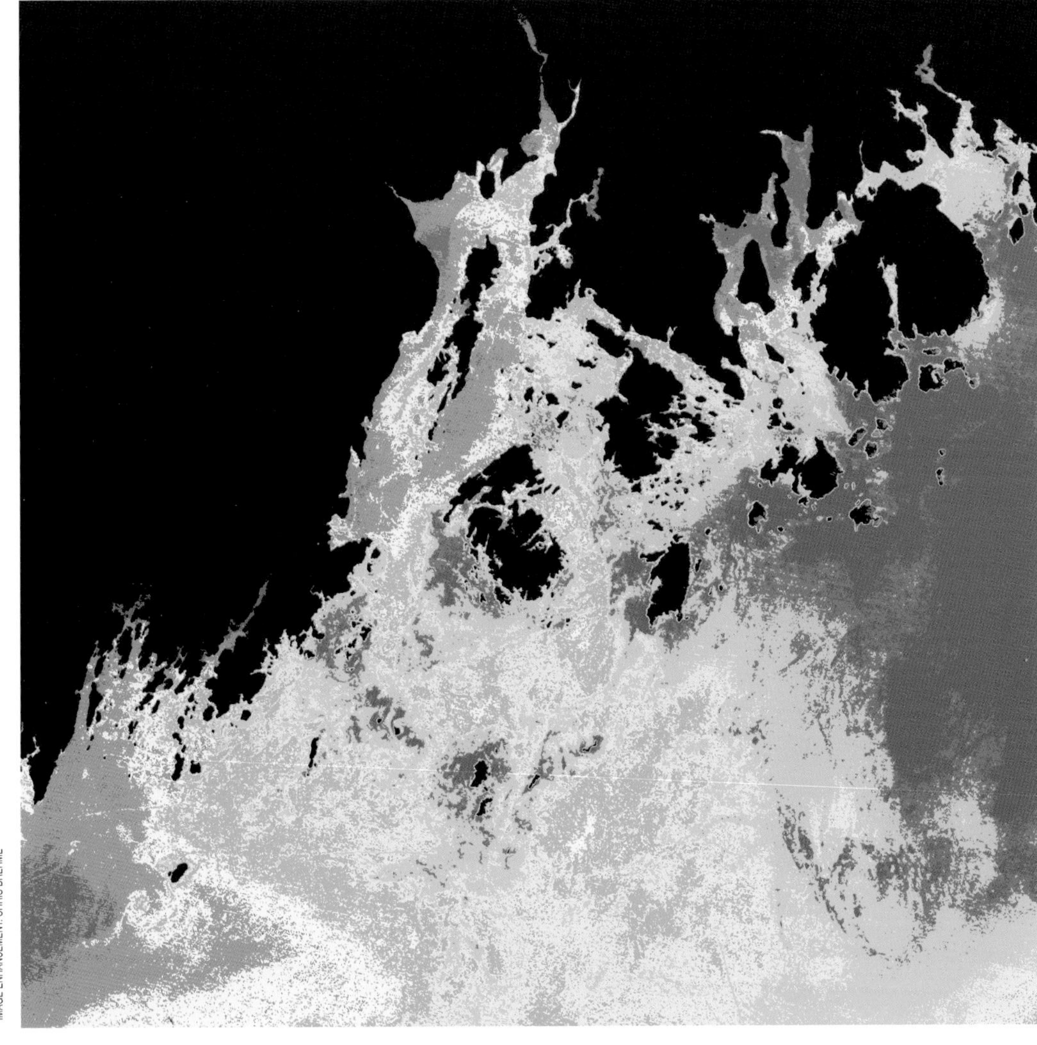

NASA's Landsat image from August 14, 1995 shows relative sea surface temperature. The thermal band from the Landsat sensor provides high resolution images of the temperature patterns in surface waters of Penobscot Bay.

Through the Penobscot Bay Project, NESDIS provided an opportunity to apply the tools of remote sensing in a comprehensive and investigative manner. The project demonstrated the applications and benefits of remote sensing in marine and coastal environments. It dramatically expanded the knowledge of the structure and function of the bay's ecosystem, and it revealed opportunities for remote sensing in studying and managing the bay and its resources. Most important, it has contributed significantly to understanding the mechanisms that affect lobsters in Penobscot Bay.

PETER RALSTON

4

Riding Coastal Currents

FINDING TINY LOBSTERS IN A VAST GULF

After uncovering the details of circulating currents and temperature fronts in the bay, a team of fishermen and scientists set out to record the patterns of lobster distribution. They wanted to find where the females that produce the eggs for the next generation of lobsters are concentrated based in part on lobstermen's observations. And they wanted to know where baby lobsters might be found in different parts of the vast Gulf of Maine

ALTHOUGH ALL OF OUR BIOLOGICAL ANCESTORS supposedly crawled out of the sea eons ago, we seem to have lost every marine instinct ever encoded in our genes. We probably know more about the intimate details of the lives of the lowliest earthworms and ants than we know about the most commercially valuable species of the world's lobsters, shrimp, cod or herring. Where are the mating or spawning grounds for marine species? How do they choose partners? Do they even have partners? Where are their eggs hatched? Where do their babies go? Where are their juvenile nursery grounds, and where do they grow into adults?

Among all these mysteries, the most difficult question, perhaps, is this: how do tiny lobsters, herring or other marine creatures, newly hatched by the thousands and millions, survive to become a small number of adults capable of reproducing themselves? Over the past five years, this question has spawned a host of projects as fishermen and scientists in the Penobscot Bay Collaborative have tried to understand lobsters' life cycle.

Where, just for starters, do the baby lobsters that grow into the astounding number of adults in the bay come from? This question is a challenge to study, because marine larvae are hard to find, even in a contained body of water such as Penobscot Bay. And tiny larvae are difficult to track from one day to the next as tides, currents and winds move water around, along with all the life it is carrying.

The obvious place to begin the arduous process of looking for larval lobsters is to understand the patterns of distribution of female lobsters - the individuals that carry the eggs that eventually are released into the confusing seas.

Ask a Lobsterman One of the most efficient means of collecting information on the distribution of egg carrying females is to ask lobstermen where they find them as they haul their traps. Sampling egg-bearing lobsters from lobster boats is called "sea sampling" and has gradually, throughout the course of the Penobscot Bay Collaborative's work, emerged into a major collaborative program of Maine's Department of Marine Resources (DMR) and hundreds of fishermen.

Since 1985 DMR has been collecting sea sampling information on the number, size, sex and other particulars of the lobsters fishermen catch, including those they return to the water. The early sampling, however, was drawn from only few areas of the coast. Between 1985 and 1997 DMR personnel would average four trips per month aboard lobster boats from three different Maine ports. In 1994, University of Maine lobster biologist Bob Steneck, along with his student Carl Wilson, began to collect similar information from lobstermen's boats along much more of the coast. This sampling was designed to address their research questions about the distribution of females and juveniles.

As a strategy to improve channels of communication between fishermen and scientists, the Penobscot Bay Collaborative decided to make a major investment in

DAVID CONOVER

Sea sampler, Carl Wilson, (above) measures an egg bearing lobster, called 'brood-stock' and the juveniles that fishermen return to the sea during the early years of the Collaborative. An adult lobster (right) regenerates a new antennae.

NICK CALOYIANIS

Carl Wilson

"YOU HAVE TO SPEND TIME OUT THERE"

Carl Wilson has fisheries science in his blood. His father, Jim Wilson, is a professor of Marine Sciences and Resource Economics at the University of Maine. "I can remember sitting on his lap during meetings when I was a kid" Wilson recalls. Carl spent his summers growing up on the Isle au Haut, and says the experience helped to shape who he is today. "You can't spend time out there without gaining an understanding of the natural environment, and a sense of how important fishing is to the community." As an undergraduate at the University of New Hampshire, Wilson studied marine biology. After graduation he became an intern at Bob Steneck's laboratory at the University of Maine's Darling Marine Center. Wilson signed on as a graduate student with Steneck and studied patterns of lobster settlement in the Gulf of Maine, and what effect they might have on overall lobster abundance. Wilson went to work at the Island Institute as a part of the Penobscot Bay Collaborative. He supervised a team of interns that were sea sampling onboard lobster boats. He also continued to monitor lobster settlement within Penobscot Bay, using SCUBA techniques, in conjunction with Steneck's team. In November of 1999 Wilson became the chief lobster biologist at the Maine Department of Marine Resources (DMR). He oversees the state's lobster monitoring program and represents Maine on interstate and federal scientific committees. He currently serves as chair of the Atlantic States Marine Fisheries Commission's lobster technical committee, which makes recommendations to the commission on lobster management and conservation proposals.

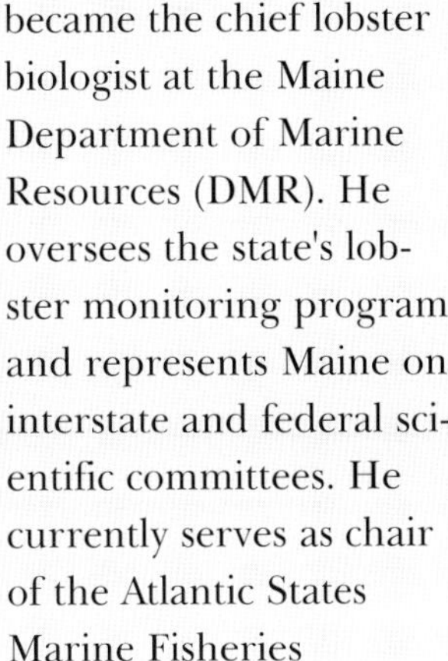

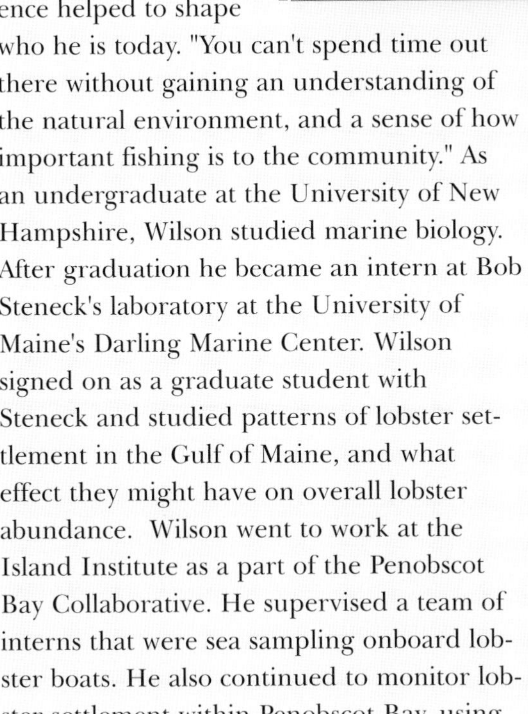

PETER RALSTON

Wilson knows about the skepticism among lobstermen about stock assessment. "Part of my job is to explain how the stock assessment process works to the industry," Wilson says, "and another part is to develop new programs in order to characterize stocks more accurately, and in ways that fishermen deal with on a daily basis." He cites the sea sampling program and the use of electronic logbooks from Thistle Marine as examples of ways fishermen can cooperate in data collection. "We plan to expand both of those programs, as well as develop long-term settlement and juvenile indices," he says.

(BN)

'Eyed' lobster eggs as they mature prior to their release into the water column.

helping to increase the number of sea samplers along the coast. In 1997, Carl Wilson joined the staff of the Island Institute to help coordinate the University of Maine's summer internship program and expand the amount of information collected aboard lobster boats. This program had two additional goals: make the data available to DMR in consistent formats, and enable lobstermen to see the results of their collective sampling efforts. The field program focused on Penobscot Bay, but also included areas in the eastern and western regions of the Maine coast.

The following year (1998), the program expanded again to include a new group called Island Fellows, who went aboard lobster boats to collect field information throughout the greater Penobscot Bay region. (The Island Fellows program of the Island Institute places recent graduates of colleges and universities in isolated communities to work on projects selected by the communities.) Island Fellows stationed in the island communities of Monhegan, Vinalhaven and Islesboro, and in the mainland town of Stonington, began to collect sea sampling data. As they did, they provided the Penobscot Bay Collaborative and the DMR with an enhanced view of the resource and the bay from the fishermen's perspective. Susan Little, the Island Institute's first Island Fellow, kept a journal, reproduced in part here, of her early days of sea sampling around the fishing grounds of Monhegan.

From Susan Little's Journal: I am taking the results of the day's sea sampling off the tape recorder: transferring the length, the sex, and molt stage, of each lobster. My voice drones out "84 ... female ... no eggs ... no notch ... old hard (shell)...," and is nearly lost among the rumble of the engine, the whine of the hauler, and Mattie Thompson's whistle over the top of it all, but its rhythm emerges, a beating pattern from within the noise. I translate my observations into numbers - the millimeters of carapace from eye socket to the base of the tail is followed by a string of zeroes and ones, symbols of presence or absence of each trait - a grid of scientific simplification.

After the first day, things become a bit more regimented. I meet Mattie and row out to his boat in the dinghy. It is cold and the sea smoke is thick on the water. We head out and quickly start hauling traps. I look up and have no idea where we are - just slipping the notch of the ruler into the eye socket and pulling it along a mottled, glossy back, turning it over to check the sex, for a notched flipper, or for eggs that looked like blackberries.

Lobsters with eggs are called "berried" females. The fishermen cut a notch in the flipper second from the right, when looking down on the lobster's back, if she has eggs. A notch means she's protected, that she is illegal to sell, so that anyone who catches her won't keep her. The berried females are put back into the water, set down on it gently out of respect for the next generation of lobsters that they hold on their bellies. The short lobsters are just tossed, too small to sell, but eggs are a mark of importance that guaranteed a careful release. We caught one really huge one, though, that I had to pick up with two hands to put back. It was a fierce looking creature and must have weighed six or seven pounds. It must have been smart to avoid all these traps for all these years.

In 1999, Maine's sea sampling program took another step forward when Carl Wilson moved to the DMR to become the state's chief lobster scientist. Already steeped in the richness of the data streams that were available from fishing boats, Wilson successfully argued for a major upgrade in effort. The DMR hired additional sea samplers to take an average of 21 trips per month from each of the seven lobster management zones off the coast. Today their information continues to be supplemented by Island Fellow sea samplers, who work in locations where it is impractical for the state to collect information.

Collectively the lobstermen's sea sampling data furnish a distinct picture. There are larger numbers of broodstock lobsters in the eastern and offshore sections of the coast of Maine. And there are higher numbers of juveniles and short lobsters in the western and inshore areas of the coast. These observations, among others, suggested what came to be known as the "larval transport" hypothesis. The abundance of lobsters in Penobscot Bay, researchers reasoned, can be attributed to the transport of floating baby lobsters from eastern Maine and Canada to the mouth of

CARL WILSON

A 'berried' female carries her eggs attached by a sticky secretion to the undersides of her tail for the better part of a year while they are developing.

Penobscot Bay via the Eastern Maine Coastal Current. Also known as the "source-sink" model, it postulates a "source" of eggs from broodstock lobsters in eastern sections of the Gulf of Maine delivered to a "sink" in the region of Penobscot Bay. Such a hypothesis was entirely consistent with the location and direction of the major circulatory currents that had been delineated and measured by both Neal Pettigrew's buoys and Andy Thomas's satellite image analysis.

Nature is usually more complicated than this, however. There are numerous ways that larvae might be retained closer to their hatching areas. So the question logically became: how much of the source is local, and how much distant? And does this change between years and over longer periods of time?

Finding Baby Lobsters The basic oceanographic work of Pettigrew and Thomas laid the groundwork for Lew Incze, a biological oceanographer at Bigelow Laboratory for Ocean Sciences, to focus on the patterns of production of baby (larval) lobsters. Are they produced in the bay from a locally retained supply of eggs (the "local retention" hypothesis) or are they transported from elsewhere? Is the answer a combination of both mechanisms, and might it vary over time?

In setting out to test the "larval transport" and "local retention" hypotheses, Incze needed to sample surface waters and map the locations of different larval stages along the coast at different times of the summer. He needed data not only in Penobscot Bay, but also in different regions of the coast to the east and west.

Incze's work as part of the Collaborative was augmented when he and Bob Steneck from the University of Maine were able to attract the interest of a graduate student, Eric Annis, in expanding the proposed larval sampling work. The idea was to identify patterns in the distribution of larval lobsters by focusing on data collection in the Eastern Maine Coastal Current and in the area west of Penobscot Bay. Annis, Incze and Steneck secured additional funding from the National Undersea Research program (NURP) and the Northeast Consortium, a cooperative research program with fishermen, funded through Sea Grant. With this additional support, the team was able to study lobster larval distribution over a wide area.

From laboratory studies, Incze and other marine biologists knew that the earliest stage of a lobster's life cycle (the egg) occurs in a relatively safe environment, under the care and protection provided by the mother lobster, as the embryos attached to her tail begin dividing and developing. Lobstermen also know from experience that in the early part of the summer, huge numbers of female lobsters head toward shore, seeking a secure location to release their eggs prior to shedding their shells.

Newly hatched lobsters ("Stage 1" larvae) rise in the water toward the surface

CHANGING DOMICILES

The cycle of shedding an old shell and growing into a new one occurs about once a year for most of the harvestable-sized lobsters in Maine waters, although shedding happens more frequently in younger lobsters and less frequently with the larger and older lobsters that are not landed in Maine. The reason lobsters shed is simple: they outgrow the fixed size of their living quarters they carry around and must crawl out of their old armor before they secrete a soft new shell that will be their chief means of protection for the ensuing year. The vast majority of all lobsters in Maine crawl into shallower, warmer waters close to shore to shed their shells. In shoal waters there are fewer predators and their growth is faster so they expand into their new shells more quickly than they would in cold water. For any particular lobster, the shedding period lasts two to three weeks but takes several months for most of the coastal lobster population as a whole to complete. The period of time right after a female sheds her old shell and during the several weeks before her new shell begins to harden is almost always the time of the year when males impregnate the females. The females crawl into the shelter of a suitable male, where they engage in "boxing" displays with their claws. Occasionally this can appear to be quite violent, but appears to be part of the bonding process. While in the male's burrow or shelter, the female signals her readiness to molt by engaging in what lobster biologists call "knighting" behavior. She places her claws on the body of the male, apparently communicating with him through an unknown pheromone or chemical means. With the male calmed down, she begins the long arduous process of wriggling out of her old shell.

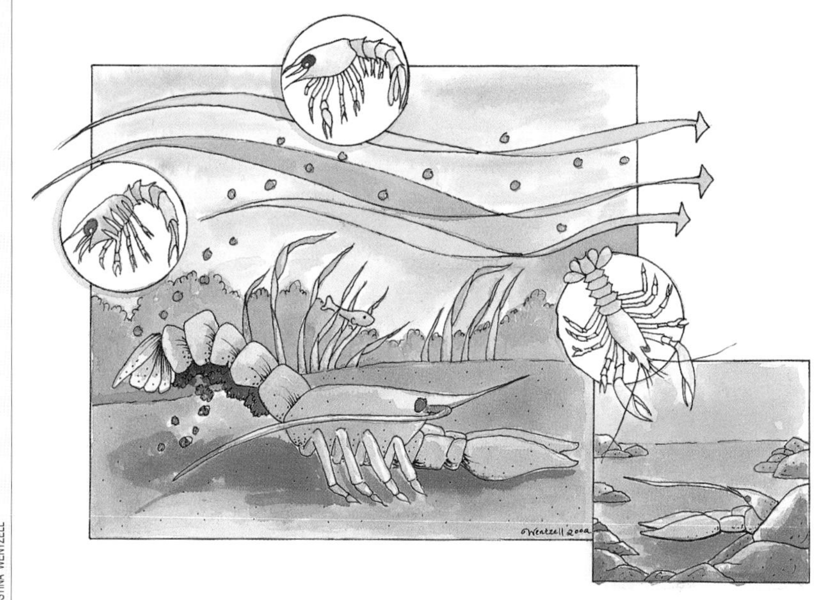

Generally within a half-hour of shedding, mating takes place. The male lobster helps turn the female over on her back and uses the last pair of legs to place a sperm packet at the entrance to the female's oviduct underneath the third pair of her tail swimmerets. (Factor, 1995).

Once a male lobster has successfully mated with a female, she will remain in his protective cover for about a week waiting for her shell to harden. Lobsters are carnivorous scavengers during most of the year, but during the "shed," they subsist on tiny planktonic food they strain through their gills. Once her shell has hardened several weeks after mating, the female lobster does something uncharacteristic of most other marine animals, except for shrimp: she begins to extrude her eggs through her oviduct where actual fertilization from male sperm occurs. As she secretes her eggs, they are coated with a gluey substance and passed along the underside of her tail by her delicate swimmerets. For the next nine to 12 months, the female will carry her eggs externally, numbering between a few thousand to a few tens of thousands in the largest females.

(PC)

Lew Incze
AT THE INTERFACE OF BIOLOGY AND PHYSICS

"To have a number of different disciplines and individuals focused on one area for five years has really produced a valuable and credible look at the mechanisms of this ecosystem," says Dr. Lew Incze, a Research Scientist at the Bigelow Laboratory for Ocean Sciences. He notes that "the value of my information has been more than doubled by the inclusion of researchers looking at the physical circulation and other life history stages of lobsters."

PETER RALSTON

Bringing together biologists, fishermen, computer modelers, oceanographers and others was a key part of the Penobscot Bay Collaborative, and this project "had a lot of the right people present," Incze says. These investigations have also led to continuing, ongoing research, which will outlast this particular project and could lead eventually to a practical and predictive population model for use in resource management.

Incze's primary research interests are in plankton ecology and fisheries oceanography. His current research focuses on larval transport, growth and survival of lobsters in the Gulf of Maine and cod on Georges Bank.

Other research projects have included pollock in the Alaska Coastal Current and King and Tanner crabs in the Bering Sea. Specifically, he works in the interface of biology and the physics of the oceans, studying how organisms are transported and react to currents, temperature fronts, eddies and turbulence. In looking at both lobsters and cod, he shares an interest with fishermen: trying to understand the production and recruitment dynamics of these two economically significant species.

As a part of the Penobscot Bay Collaborative, Incze studied the production, development and distribution of the planktonic stages of lobster throughout the summer season. This information has helped establish a connection between planktonic and settled benthic populations. Incze has also collaborated in a study that followed lobster supply and settlement at a site in Rhode Island, providing a look at the ecology of the same organism in a notably different oceanographic setting.

For all the answers it produced, the Penobscot Bay Collaborative has also raised many questions about the ecology of lobsters in the bay and beyond, particularly involving issues of local vs. distant larval supply and understanding the large changes observed in larval abundance. Incze plans to continue larval monitoring in Penobscot Bay, but also notes that "the answer to the question of where the larvae come from, which we continue to investigate, is further complicated due to the fact that the origin of larvae in any area can change from year to year with oceanographic conditions." (BN)

where they are visible to the naked eye, but they are generally hidden in the vastness of the water column. These planktonic lobsters will float for the next 20 or more days as they develop through three more floating stages. Able to swim relatively short distances, these tiny lobsters are largely carried by the vagaries of the ocean's currents. Eventually, at "Stage 4," they develop small claws and look just like miniatures of the familiar adult form one sees on a dinner plate. These fully equipped little lobsters, ready to settle to the bottom, are called "post-larvae" because they are so distinct from the previous three larval stages.

Tiny Patterns in Space Incze set up a series of transects that radiated like spokes from the hub of the mid-Penobscot Bay islands of Vinalhaven and North Haven. Each transect consisted of numerous stations. Field work involved towing a fine-mesh plankton net of specific dimensions alongside a boat moving at a slow but constant speed along a given course at each station. After each tow, the contents of the net were emptied and the lobster larvae, if any, were counted. Different stages of the lobster provided important clues to where the lobsters hatched.

In 1999, from the end of June to the beginning of September, Incze and his team surveyed Penobscot Bay every week. In 2000 they added two transects in outer Penobscot Bay. Meanwhile Annis set up transects across the Eastern Maine Coastal Current, beginning west of Penobscot Bay and all along the eastern coast of Maine to Grand Manan Island in Canada.

The first two years of Incze's and Annis's larval sampling work reveal important

NICK CALOYIANIS

Mature lobster eggs ready to be released into ocean currents.

Stage 1 larva of the American lobster side view and top view, age 3 days.

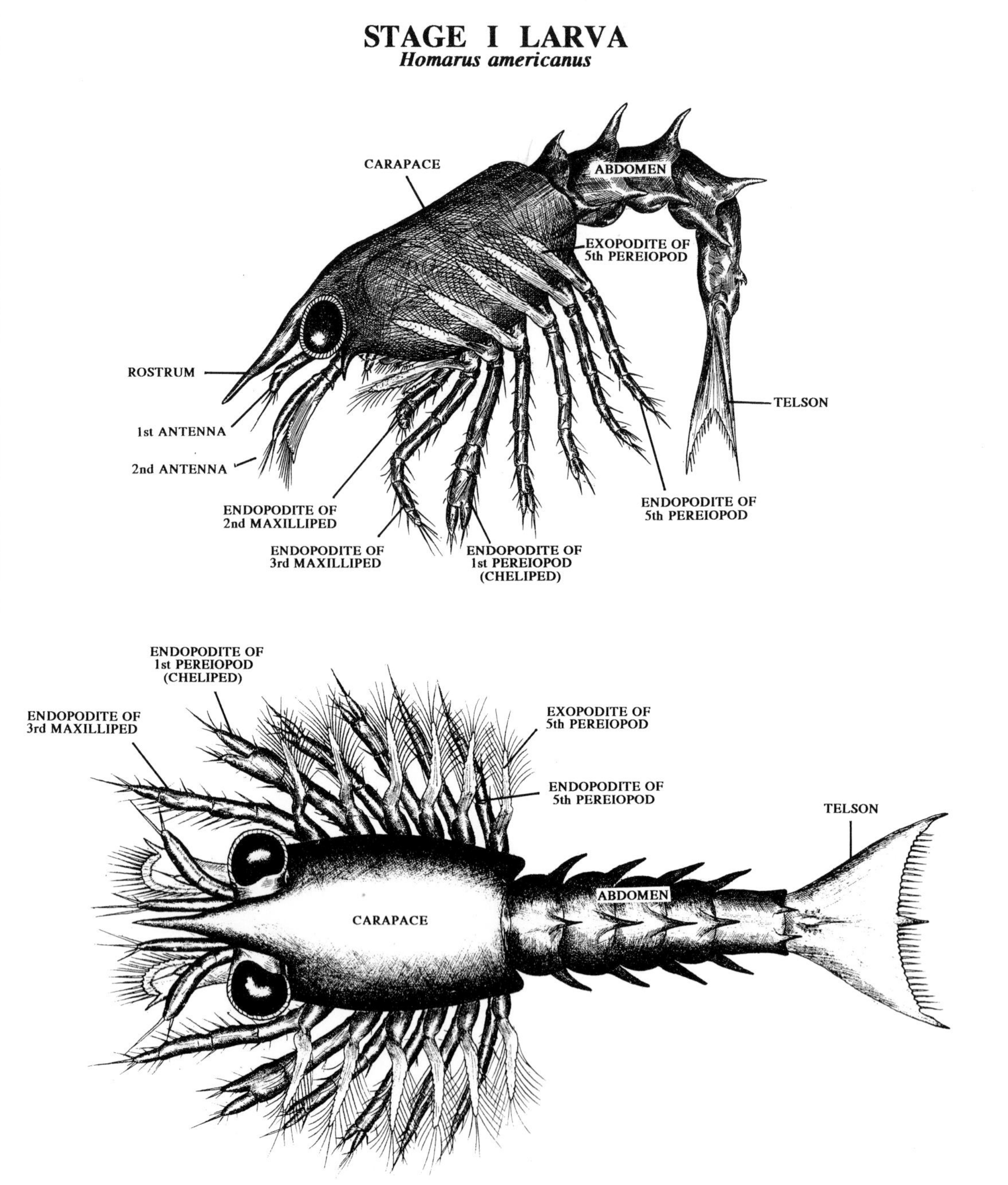

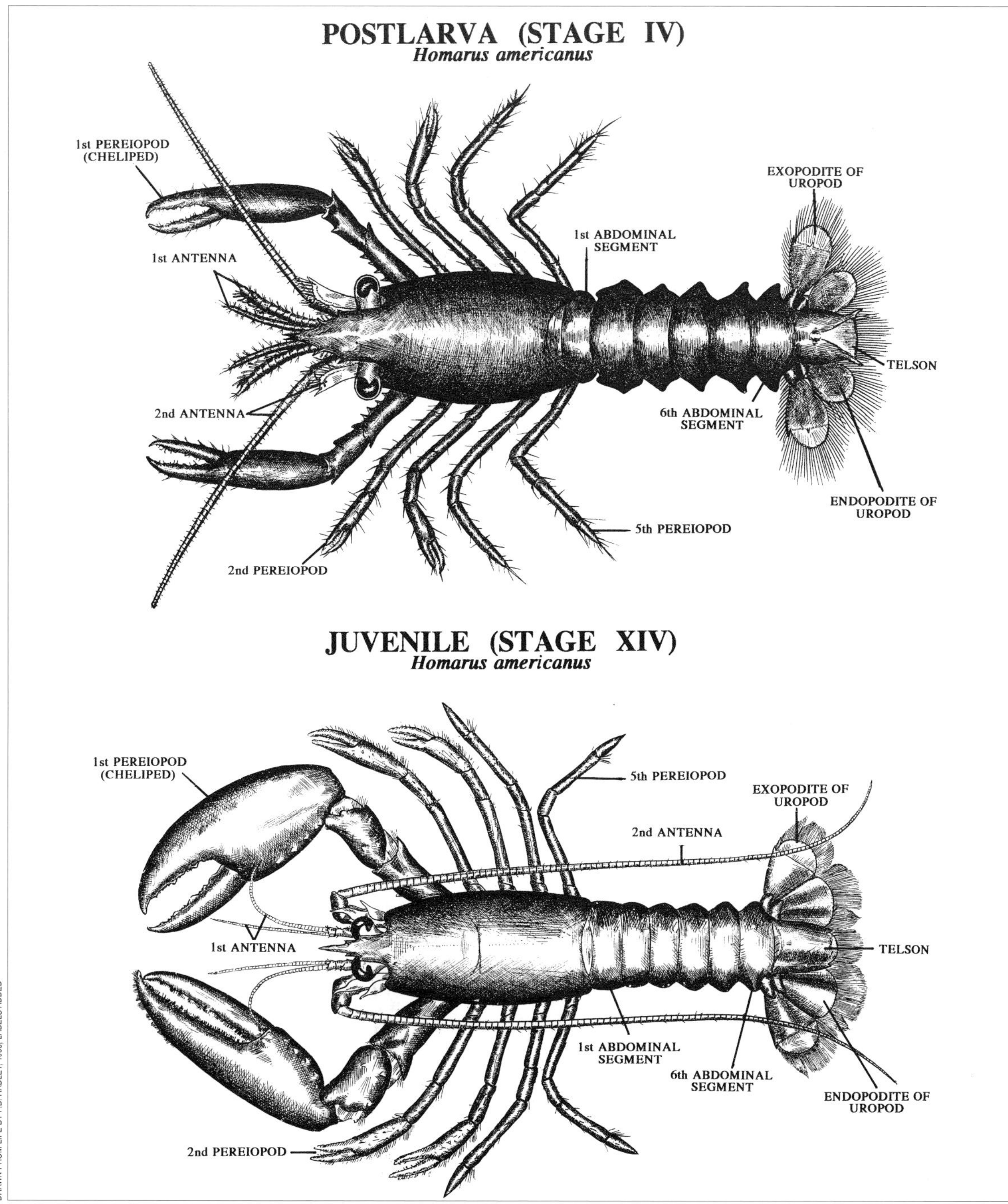

DRAWN FROM LIFE BY P.B. HADLEY, 1906, LABELS ADDED

Top: Stage 4 postlarva before it settles to the bottom, age 14 days. (Bottom) juvenile lobster, age 14 months,0 approximately 2-3 inches in length.

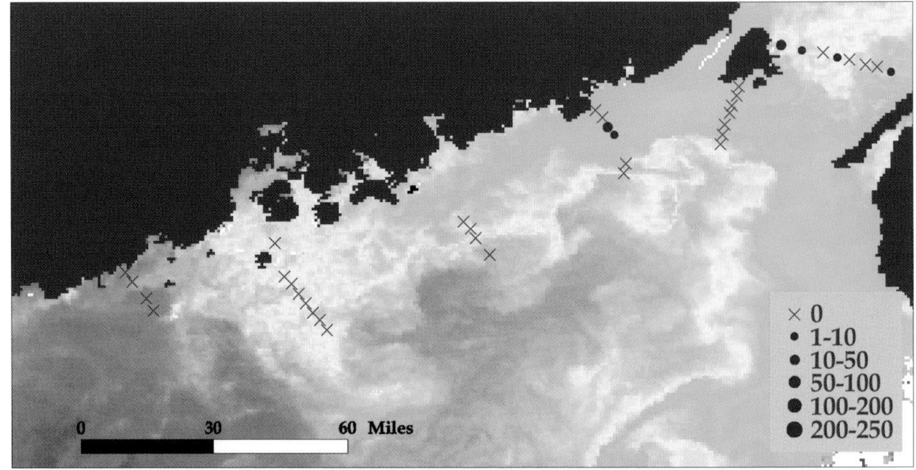

The distribution of Stage 1 larval lobsters from the 1999 cruise displayed on a sea surface temperature image of a typical summer day showing early stage lobsters located primarily at the outer edge of the Eastern Maine Coastal Current.

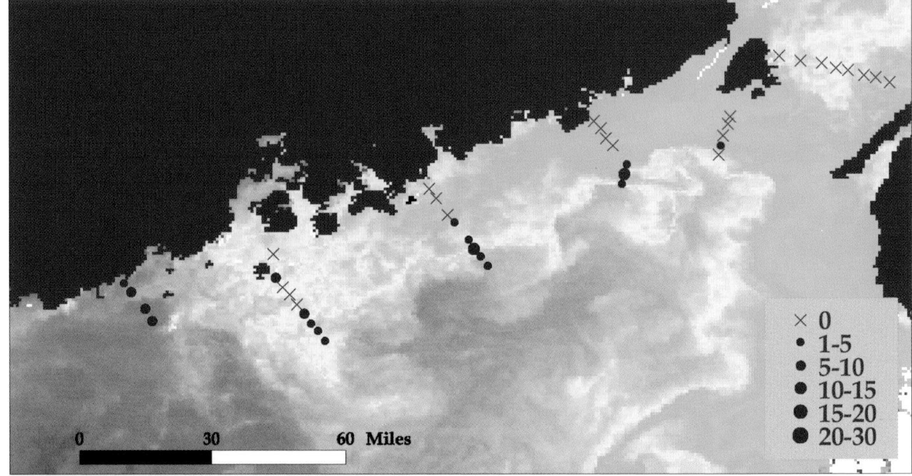

The distribution of Stage 1 larval lobsters from the 2001 cruise showing a concentration of early stage lobsters produced at Grand Manan Island in Canada and along much of the length of the Eastern Maine Coastal Current, extending westward along the shores to Casco Bay.

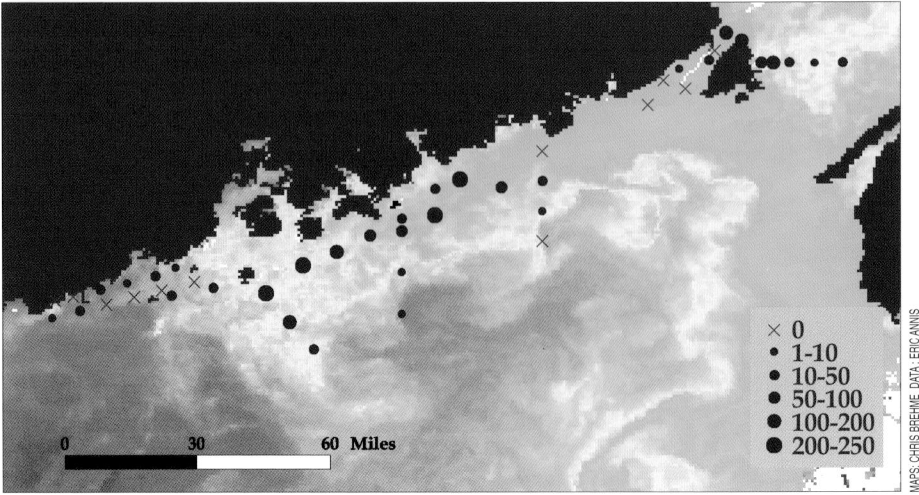

The distribution of Stage 4 larval lobsters from the 2001 cruise showing late stage lobsters riding in the Eastern Maine Coastal Current and concentrating in the region near the mouth of Penobscot Bay and along the shores to the westward.

MAPS: CHRIS BREHME DATA: ERIC ANNIS

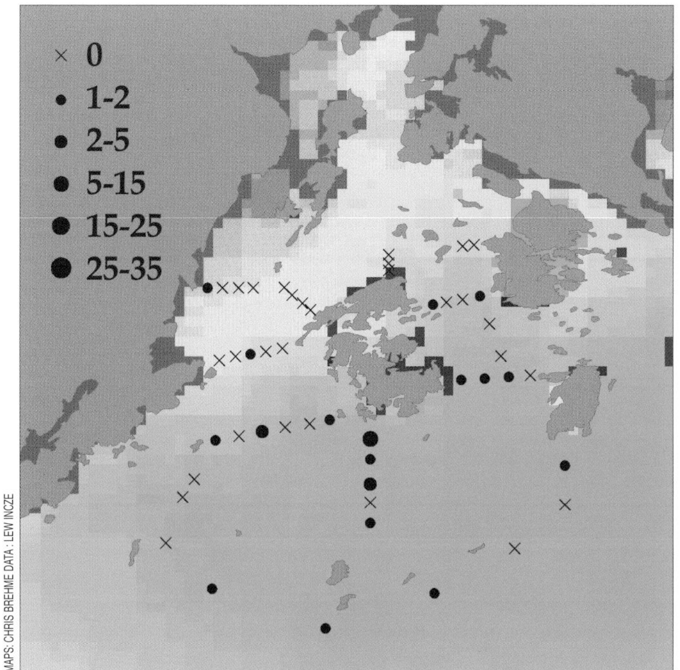

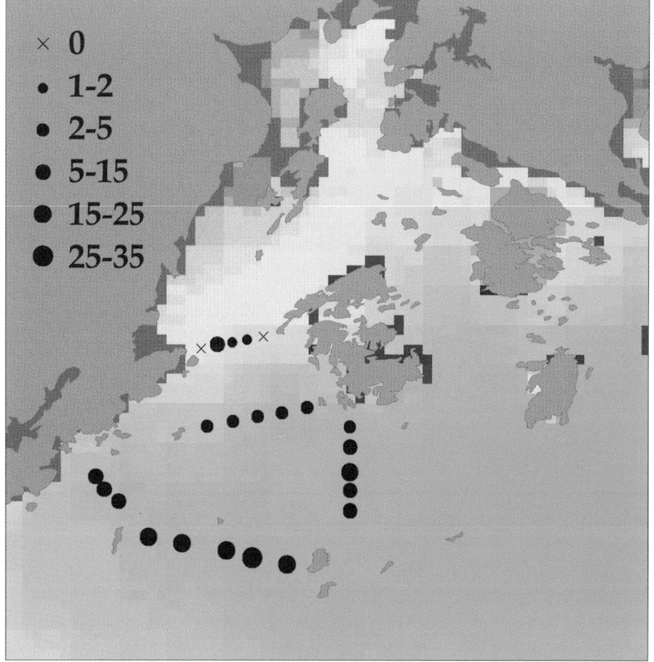

MAPS: CHRIS BREHME DATA: LEW INCZE

Stage 4 larval lobster distribution in Penobscot Bay in 1999 (left) and 2001 (right) showing greatly increased numbers of larvae in 2001. The distribution in both years reveals that the outer bay has late stage larvae even in a low larval production year. In a high larval production year, larvae are found around the ring of the mid bay islands, but not in the northern bay.

patterns. The first fact that emerges from the larval tows is that both Stage 1 and Stage 4 larvae were present - but Stage 2 and Stage 3 were nearly absent. This result was not surprising, since other researchers have also failed to find any of these life stages in surface waters. Together the observations suggest that Stage 2 and Stage 3 lobsters descend lower in the water column.

Annis found Stage 1 lobster larvae present all along the Eastern Maine Coastal Current during both the 1999 and 2001 field seasons. He also noted, during both years, a large concentration of Stage 1 larvae off Grand Manan Island at the eastern end of the Eastern Maine Coastal Current. Earlier underwater videos of large female lobsters in a concentrated area in the waters off Grand Manan had shown that females there actually excavate nests in the soft muddy bottom, from which they release their eggs. Over a period of days to a week, these large egg-carrying females stir little water eddies with their swimmerets under their tails, causing the egg membranes to rupture, releasing the newly hatched larval lobsters.

Another spike of Stage 1 lobsters is found at the mouth of Penobscot Bay, indicating the possible presence of another concentration of local broodstock there. Annis's sampling of the Eastern Maine Coastal Current during the 2000 field season revealed relatively few Stage 4 lobsters in Eastern Maine, although he did not sample intensively close to the shore. Nevertheless, there is a strong spatial pattern of the presence of post-larvae, beginning at the western edges of Penobscot Bay and extending westward to Casco Bay. These are also areas of dense and extensive broodstock, unlike the unusual pattern of concentrated broodstock lobsters found in a relatively confined area off North Head, Grand Manan.

Larval Deliveries Incze's larval surveys in Penobscot Bay provided the intensity of seasonal coverage

NICK CALOYIANIS

required to sample all life stages properly, and revealed important details of the general pattern detected in Annis' field work. Incze's survey pattern - spokes around the hub of Vinalhaven-North Haven - was set up to test the hypothesis that larvae are carried on currents up the western side of the bay.

In Incze's surveys, Stage 1 and Stage 4 larvae were in fact found in those waters where the Eastern Maine Coastal Current is strongest, at the mouth of Penobscot Bay and up its western edge, where a part of the coastal current turns inshore. Also, Incze found no larvae of any stage north of North Haven. This pattern corresponds to the patterns revealed in the sea sampling data: the further north one goes in the bay, the fewer juveniles. Juveniles are most abundant in the outer and western portions of the bay, where the number of Stage 4 lobsters is also greatest. Perhaps the fishing is less lucrative in the northern bay because the number of baby lobsters arriving there is limited. And possibly the number of baby lobsters is limited because the outer coastal currents that have carried them to the mouth of the bay do not penetrate with great force to its northern reaches. So far, so good for the "introduction" or "advection" hypothesis.

But there is a major difficulty with this hypothesis. Neal Pettigrew's oceanographic buoy data show that surface waters are flowing south out of the bay during the period when Stage 1 and Stage 4 larvae are floating and/or swimming in the waters near the mouth of the bay. Perhaps the large numbers of Stage 1 and Stage 4 larvae in the lower bay do not indicate that they were brought there by the Eastern Maine Coastal Current after all; perhaps they were produced in the bay and then flushed on the surface gyres into the outer bay.

As in Annis's surveys, Incze found no Stage 2 or 3 lobster larvae at all, because they are riding currents lower in the water column that were not sampled by the surface tows. Until we have a good understanding of the patterns of distribution of Stage 2 and 3 larvae, it will not be possible to sort out the introduction-advection hypothesis from the local retention hypothesis. Annis's field work during the 2001 field season expand-

PETER RALSTON

Colorful crustacean in its habitat (facing page) and lobster skiff at Friendship..

ed his survey work to the regions "downstream" or down-current from Penobscot Bay, where he added 12 stations between Port Clyde and Cape Small. When Annis grouped his western samples into offshore and inshore components, he found that over three times as many post-larvae appear in inshore regions, as opposed to offshore areas. While the mechanism that explains the inshore position of post-larvae as they are simultaneously moving west is not clear, the pattern is nevertheless striking.

Another interesting and suggestive finding from the field data, detected by both Incze and Annis, is the common appearance of two peaks in the abundance of post-larvae in the western sections of Penobscot Bay and coastal regions to the westward. The first occurs in July, probably from local production. Then, approximately two weeks later, a secondary peak appears. This second peak may be from larvae that are carried or "advected" from farther away, possibly on coastal currents from eastern Maine. Whatever the sources of these two peaks, post-larvae ready to settle to the bottom begin to appear and are most abundant west of the persistent temperature front between the cooler waters of eastern Maine and the warmer waters west of Penobscot Bay. This temperature front, reported since Henry Bigelow's day, was revealed by Andy Thomas's analysis of a 12-year archive of satellite images of sea surface temperatures. It suggests that larval lobsters are responding to subtle temperature cues as they mature and prepare to change their lives from floating plankton to a life on the bottom.

The important point to emphasize, however, is that there are two possible explanations for the abundance of larvae and post-larvae in the warmer surface water regions west of the persistent Penobscot Bay temperature front that satellite-borne sensors routinely detect. Either larvae aggregate in this region because early stage larvae arrive there on the Eastern Maine Coastal Current from a lengthy section of the Maine coast, and then develop in large numbers as the currents slow down in the convergence zone west of the front - or, if the Eastern Maine Coastal Current is diverted offshore upon reaching the region of Penobscot Bay, the post-larvae in the area could come from local hatching and from the production supplied from west Penobscot Bay. Oceanographers have not yet resolved the current structure in outer Penobscot Bay in sufficient detail to say for certain. But new tools under development and recently deployed in Penobscot Bay may provide the "smoking gun" needed to answer the larval delivery question in the very near future (see Chapter 7).

Preliminary Findings In biological investigations, especially in the ever-changing conditions of the marine environment, two years of field data are not sufficient for firm conclusions. Whether larval lobsters in Penobscot Bay are produced elsewhere and delivered here by ocean currents, or whether they are produced in the bay and retained by local currents, is still too uncertain to sort out definitively. During the summer of 2000, the number of larval lobsters sampled along most of the Maine coast (as well as in places more distant such as the sampling station at the Seabrook nuclear power plant in New Hampshire) hit an all-time low. In fact, other studies conducted by Incze and his colleague Rick Wahle at Bigelow have shown that larval lobster numbers along sections of the western Maine coast have been declining since 1995. But then, during the 2001 field season, lobster larval numbers rebounded to near record highs.

Because of these variations—very low larval supplies followed by very high numbers of larvae—it is not yet possible to be definitive about the mechanisms of larval supply in Penobscot Bay. Because post-larvae are in surface waters, they can exit from Penobscot Bay from either the east or west bays. They are more abundant in the west bay than the east, and the buoy and wind data for the two years of sampling tell us these post-larvae are on their way out of the bay. Still, no one knows for certain how many earlier stage lobsters are entering the bay, because no one has yet sampled to find out where in the water column the intermediate Stage 2 and Stage 3 larvae are, and what currents they are riding. This work is planned for the summer of 2002.

And to make things a little more complicated, it is also possible that a combination of larval transport from the east and local production from the bay is at work. The take-away message for the time being is that wild fluctuations in larval lobster numbers are a strong indication that egg production and larval supply are largely decoupled, due to the strong role oceanographic factors play in controlling where larvae go.

It may seem as if the scientists haven't learned much. Nothing could be further from the truth. The lobster scientists have learned that there are no simple solutions to the riddles of lobster distribution and abundance, but they have learned what life stages they must now focus on. Most significantly, they know when and where to look. As they do, the researchers and their collaborating fishermen are tantalizingly close to answers.

PETER RALSTON

5

Where Lobsters Rain

CONDOS UNDER COBBLES AND BOULDERS

FOR MORE THAN A CENTURY, biologists have known that newly hatched lobsters spend the first three or four weeks of their larval lives floating on ocean currents. Lobster larvae get to be stronger swimmers week by week as they go through a series of metamorphic changes in their external anatomy. By the time they have developed all the external body parts and look like fully formed tiny lobsters, they have become what lobster biologists call "post-larvae." Once lobsters reach this phase, their lives radically change from a water-borne or planktonic existence to a benthic or bottom-dwelling one, for the rest of their lives.

After floating for weeks on coastal currents that circulate in and out of the bays of Maine, baby lobsters dive to the bottom to find protective niches where they will spend the next years of their lives. No one knows what causes lobsters to head for the bottom, but lobster biologists and lobstermen both know that lobsters are exceptionally attuned to changing water temperatures and much more prevalent in certain areas of a bay than others. Trying to explain these patterns became an important focus of members of the Collaborative.

No one really knows what compels these fully equipped, miniature lobsters about the length of a fingernail to leave the water column and head for the bottom. Really the only way to understand this all-important transition is to don wetsuits and slip beneath the surface to find where the youngest of the young lobsters settle on the bottom.

The "settlement" phase of a young lobster's life is crucially important to biologists, because once these lobsters reach suitable cover on the sea bottom, their lives and patterns of distribution become easier to predict.

Over a decade ago, Rick Wahle of the Bigelow Laboratory for Ocean Sciences developed a new method of counting these newly settled tiny lobsters. By hooking a SCUBA tank to a six-foot length of PVC plumbing tube with a mesh bag at the end, Wahle created a sort of underwater vacuum cleaner that was able to suction up the contents of complex micro-habitats and reliably count the number of newly settled tiny lobsters in different nursery habitats.

Heading to the Bottom Wahle and Steneck coined the term "early benthic phase" to describe this early period in a lobster's life. According to their painstaking detective work, tiny lobsters are not uniformly distributed over all types of bottom, but are found in much higher numbers in specialized habitats. Wahle, Steneck and numerous others have shown that post-larval lobsters are somehow programmed to seek out and settle in cobble and boulder environments or in other complex habitats where natural shelters abound. Settling lobsters actively avoid sandy or muddy bottoms.

In terms of their geometric complexity, cobble and boulder habitats are the ecological equivalent of coral reefs. The complex and intricate micro-topography offers an abundance of different nooks and crannies that provide protective shelter for young lobsters where they will spend the next few years of their lives. As early benthic phase lobsters grow from fingernail to finger size, they can move from shelter to shelter, rarely exposing themselves to the hazards of predation.

From work completed by Carl Wilson, we also know that most post-larvae along the Maine coast settle in shallow waters (less than 60 feet) and most of them in waters of less than 30 feet. Since shallow coastal waters are also the warmest, some biologists have speculated that post-larval lobsters respond to warmer temperatures that trigger them to dive to the bottom. Other researchers have reported observing tiny lobsters at the cusp of the change in their lives making repeated exploratory dives to the bottom, apparently looking for suitable habitat.

Lobster biologist Diane Cowan of The Lobster Conservancy, based in

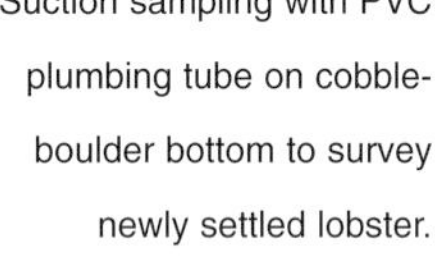

Suction sampling with PVC plumbing tube on cobble-boulder bottom to survey newly settled lobster.

COURTESY RICK WAHLE

Friendship, Maine, has developed a novel technique to survey patterns of newly settled lobsters. Once a month, when the lowest of low tides uncovers the lower intertidal zone, Cowan has reliably found various sizes of lobsters from the smallest settlers to quite large juveniles. The Lobster Conservancy has developed a network of volunteers to survey a significant number of subtidal sites along the New England coast to determine patterns of settlement, using her relatively inexpensive sampling technique.

Benthic Habitats In order to understand the availability and distribution of suitable habitat for early benthic phase and juvenile lobsters, the Penobscot Bay Collaborative funded a two-year program to map the bottom habitats in Penobscot Bay. Joe Kelley, the state's marine geologist and a researcher at the University of Maine, along with his colleagues, has been mapping underwater habitats along the Maine coast for many years. Kelley proposed using side-scanning sonar to generate maps of the bottom of Penobscot Bay. This area had never before been systematically described.

Up until the last few decades, virtually all benthic habitat mapping depended on "bottom grabs" of one type or another. A researcher would lower a device to collect a scoop or a core of the bottom consisting of mud, sand, shell, gravel, rock or some combination of these substrates. The results of each bottom grab would be noted and transferred to a map, ultimately producing a series of point descriptions that might be generalized into habitats literally by connecting the dots.

The shortcomings of this approach are obvious. One marine researcher likened this technique to trying to describe the terrestrial landscape from a hovering hot air balloon on a foggy day, by lowering buckets to earth's surface and trying to interpret the results from what is retrieved.

Kelley and colleague Steve Dickson, however, have become experts in interpreting side-scan sonar imagery originally developed by the U.S. Navy for submarine navigation. Using a towed "fish" equipped with sonar, researchers bounce a series of sonic waves off the bottom. Various textures of the

NICK CALOYIANIS

The number of eggs a large female lobster carries increases exponentially with age. This relationship between age and fecundity is a compelling biological rationale for the prohibition on landing large lobsters in Maine.

Bob Steneck

"THE BEST PLACE ON THE PLANET TO STUDY LOBSTERS"

Dr. Robert Steneck, Professor of Marine Sciences at the University of Maine, has spent thousands of hours underwater since his first dive in 1960 at age ten. In his research into coral ecology, plant-herbivore interactions and, of course, lobsters, he has been in waters ranging from warm tropical seas to the cold rocky coastline of Maine. Until the Penobscot Bay project, he had for the most part avoided embayments, but the interesting conditions of Penobscot Bay caused him to reconsider.

PETER RALSTON

"There is a distinct break in the gradient of lobster abundance present along the Maine coastline at Penobscot Bay," he says. "Lobster population densities east of Penobscot Bay are much lower than those west of the bay, so I decided to have a better look at what was in the bay." At the mouth of the bay, it was immediately apparent to Steneck why this area has long been known for its superlative harvests. "I thought I knew what a lot of lobsters looked like," he says, "but here we saw densities that blew everything else out of the water."

Steneck notes the many factors that come together in the Gulf of Maine, including the cycle of yearly temperature changes and the high primary productivity of the waters that make this "the best place on the planet to study lobsters."

As a part of this project, Steneck and his team of graduate students and interns logged hundreds of dives counting both large and small lobsters on selected patches of bottom, primarily to determine the abundance and distribution of newly settled lobsters. He also sought to determine where the larvae were coming from, by learning to quantify the distribution and abundance of large egg-bearing lobsters with submarines and remotely operated vehicles. The settlement data, along with the oceanographic work of graduate student Eric Annis and other researchers in the collaborative, has led to the theory that the abundance of newly settled lobsters in the mouth of Penobscot Bay results from both the retention of developing larvae hatched in the bay and larvae transported via the Eastern Maine Coastal

Current. "I suspect this may be the 'larvae superhighway' for the settlement we've been seeing in western Penobscot Bay," he notes. Steneck hopes that this information can be used directly for management in the future. "If you can quantify settlement, as we now can do with greater accuracy, then you can make predictions of harvest," he says.

To have an effectively co-managed fishery, Steneck says, one must monitor two separate biological signals. Managers are primarily interested in ensuring long-term health of the stock by maintaining a robust, reproducing broodstock, and the fishermen are primarily interested in ensuring that there are new animals entering the population and thus keeping the harvestable population levels high. By understanding and monitoring both the number of large breeding lobsters and the number of larvae (and thus new animals), managers are able to keep populations and harvests at healthy levels. Steneck believes the Penobscot Bay Marine Collaborative has "brought some clarity to both of these elements, and helped put our finger on the pulse of Maine lobster populations."
(BN)

Habitat types of the sea floor off mid-coast Maine: muddy bottoms (brown); rock ledge habitats (beige); sandy habitats (red) and gravel and cobble bottoms (olive--green).

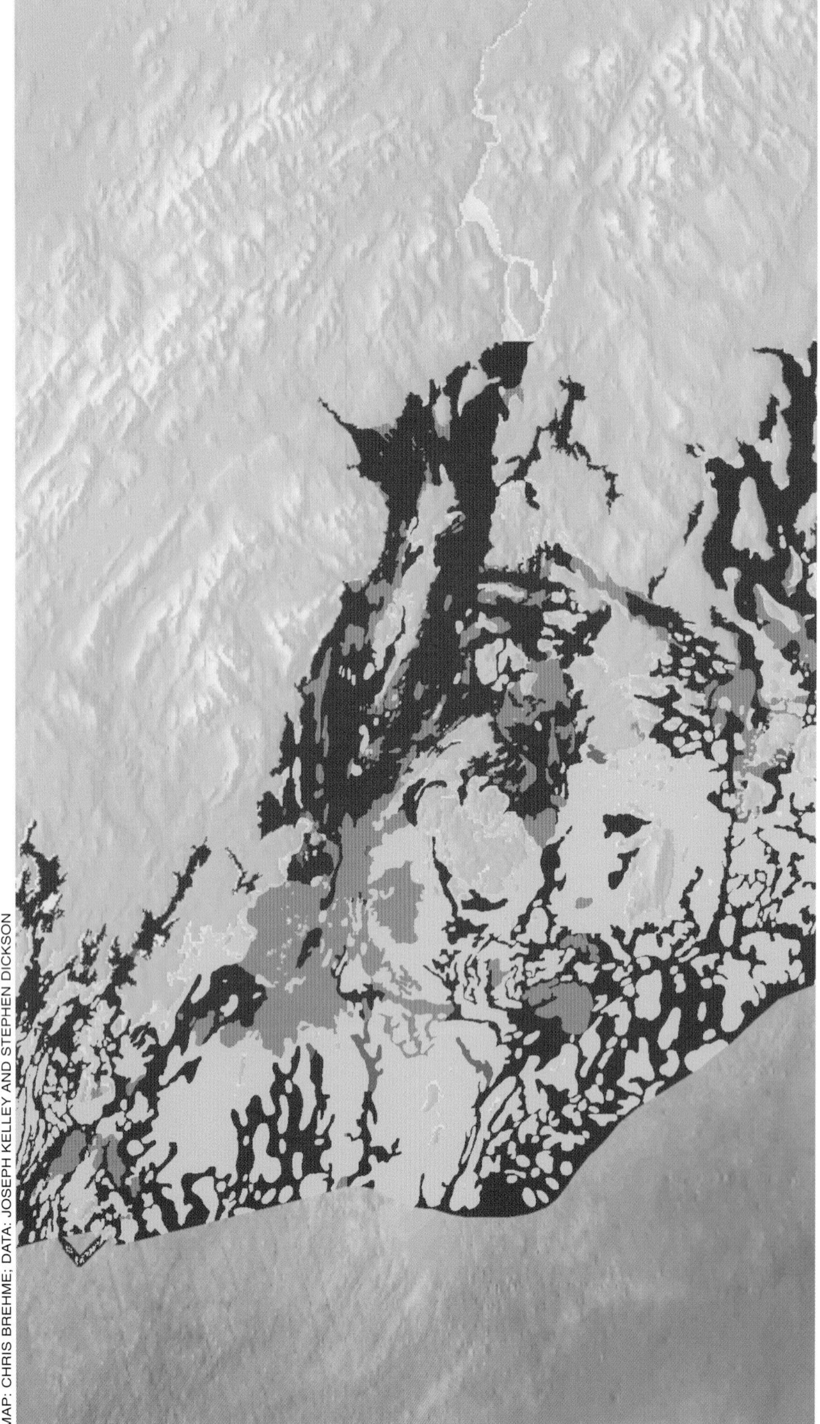
MAP: CHRIS BREHME; DATA: JOSEPH KELLEY AND STEPHEN DICKSON

bottom produce different sonic echoes that are distinctive: mud, sand, gravel, boulders, ledges. In a single transect, side-scanning sonar images produce as much information as could be collected during a year using bottom grabs.

Because the towed "fish" automatically keeps track of its position over the bottom through a global positioning system (GPS) unit, Kelley is able to correlate the sonar images with precise locations. The imagery is much richer in detail than can be incorporated into a map. Kelley and Dickson, therefore, convert the imagery into habitat maps that group the data by its primary component - sand, mud, gravel (cobble) or rock. Roughly half of Penobscot Bay's vast underwater topography was sampled, using side-scanning sonar techniques.

The picture of the bottom that emerges shows that in Penobscot Bay, mud is the dominant habitat. Mud bottom comprises over half of the bay's bottom, mostly in deep water sections of east and west Penobscot Bays and trending out to the outermost southwestern parts of the bay. Sandy bottom environments are found in the outer portion of west Penobscot Bay, perhaps remnants of Penobscot River deposits and outwash deltas produced when the sea level was lower and the vast

Joe Kelley:

RESEARCH WITH WIDER IMPLICATIONS

NAKOMIS NELSON

Joseph Kelley, Ph.D., used sidescan sonar, a remotely operated video camera and analysis of sediment samples to describe the bottom of Penobscot Bay. This information, more accurate and detailed than any previously collected, has resulted in a map of the sediments and rock types found throughout the bay. The map, in turn, has been used to measure the amount of appropriate lobster habitat in the bay and its role as a limiting factor for Penobscot Bay's lobster population. Involvement in the issues of the day is nothing new for Kelley, a marine geologist at the University of Maine. He is interested in the effects of sea-level change on shorelines and has been active in discussions along the coast regarding the effects of dredging, beach nourishment, jetties and sea walls on both built and natural environments.

"I enjoy working on basic scientific research problems that have societal implications," he says.

Kelley's work for the Penobscot Bay Collaborative has allowed him to pursue another interest: the gigantic "pockmark" formations in the muddy sediments of Belfast Bay, in the northern reaches of Penobscot Bay. The round formations apparently occur when pockets of methane gas beneath the surface grow to a certain size. Methane escapes with a violent eruption, leaving a pockmark behind.

(AH)

Sidescan sonar image of Foley Ledge, Vinalhaven

glaciers that once covered the Penobscot watershed were melting. The cobble and boulder habitats that are crucial to the survival of early benthic phase and juvenile lobsters are abundant in the region south of Vinalhaven and around the edges of virtually all of the islands throughout the bay. One of the questions that the habitat maps of benthic environments allows us to ask is how the available habitat for newly settled lobsters is distributed throughout Penobscot Bay. Or, phrased another way: Are the specialized cobble and boulder habitats that are so important for early benthic phase lobsters a limiting factor for lobster populations?

Chris Brehme, a GIS expert at the Island Institute, combined two layers of geographic information in the bay, including gravel and rocky bottom habitats from the Kelley data, and overlaid this information on areas where the water depth is less than 60 feet. Using this technique, he could illustrate the distribution of potentially favorable settlement habitat throughout the bay. A quick look at the resulting map shows that settlement habitat for lobsters is abundant throughout all regions of the bay. If a picture is worth a thousand words, a map can be worth ten thousand.

Hot Spots, Cold Spots Recognizing that favorable settlement habitat may not be a significant limiting factor in Penobscot Bay, researchers in the Collaborative then set out to find where lobsters actually settle. Steneck and his students at University of Maine's Darling Center were already using SCUBA diving techniques to study the patterns of lobster distribution throughout different life stages. Prior to the establishment of the Collaborative, they had been monitoring a series of underwater sites to the east and west of Penobscot Bay to collect information on the distribution of lobsters in their early life phases. These early phases—new settlers, early benthic and adolescent phase - describe the first five or six years of a lobster's life, before they enter the fishery. In 1998, Steneck expanded his study to Penobscot Bay, to study high-resolution patterns there and to correlate his team's findings with the oceanographic, satellite imaging and benthic mapping work done by others.

To monitor newly settled lobsters on the bottom of the bay, Steneck and his colleagues located sites in waters of 30 feet or less on cobble and boulder bottoms similar to those they had studied between York and Jonesport, Maine, since 1989. They chose sites in southwest-facing coves because Wahle's and Incze's work had earlier shown that southwesterly breezes are important factors in delivering larvae to shallow water nursery habitats. In Penobscot Bay, Steneck established 44 benthic sampling sites, in all regions of the bay.

In order to find the smallest early benthic phase lobsters in their small crevice refugia, Steneck and his divers employed Wahle's suction technique to vacuum small particles and organisms from half-meter square quadrats. Complementing these intensively sampled suction sites were larger, meter-square quadrats where lobsters were counted visually. Although visual counts in the larger quadrats didn't reveal the smallest early benthic phase lobsters buried in crevices, divers could reliably spot claws, antennae or burrow entrances that indicated their presence. The researchers also reported that lobsters larger than finger size were usually sufficiently curious to show themselves to divers before retreating by tail-flipping back into their burrows. Hand-sized boulders could also be moved or removed within each quadrat to permit the location, capture and measurement of all lobsters in the quadrat.

The high resolution sampling in Penobscot Bay revealed distinct areas of high and low settlement of small lobsters. Steneck refers to these as "hot spots" and "cold spots." Penobscot Bay's lobster settlement hot spot stretched from the southwestern mouth of the bay and widened to the west. The settlement cold spot exists in the northeastern section of the bay and extends asymmetrically south, down east Penobscot Bay. The subsurface sampling data reveal a similar pattern among larger, older adolescent-phase lobsters which have the highest population densities in the vicinity of settlement hot spots and much lower densities throughout most of the cold spot regions.

Steneck and Wilson's "hot" and "cold" spot findings from their benthic sampling program can be interpreted as supporting the hypothesis that lobster larvae are delivered to the region of the mouth of Penobscot Bay by the Eastern Maine Coastal Current. The settlement hot spots correspond closely to an oceanographic "front," revealed by satellite imagery, where the Eastern Maine Coastal Current turns

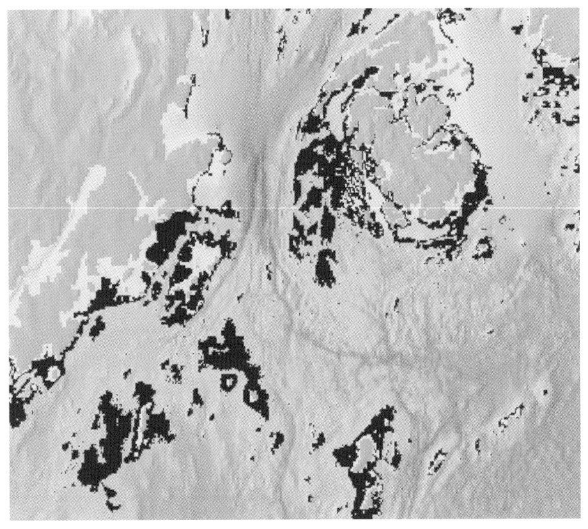

Potential lobster settlement habitat along the midcoast region of Maine (below) with detail (above) showing settlement habitat in Penobscot Bay. The areas highlighted in dark blue are rocky- ledge and gravel-cobble bottoms in less than 60 feet of water favored by a large majority of newly-settled lobsters.

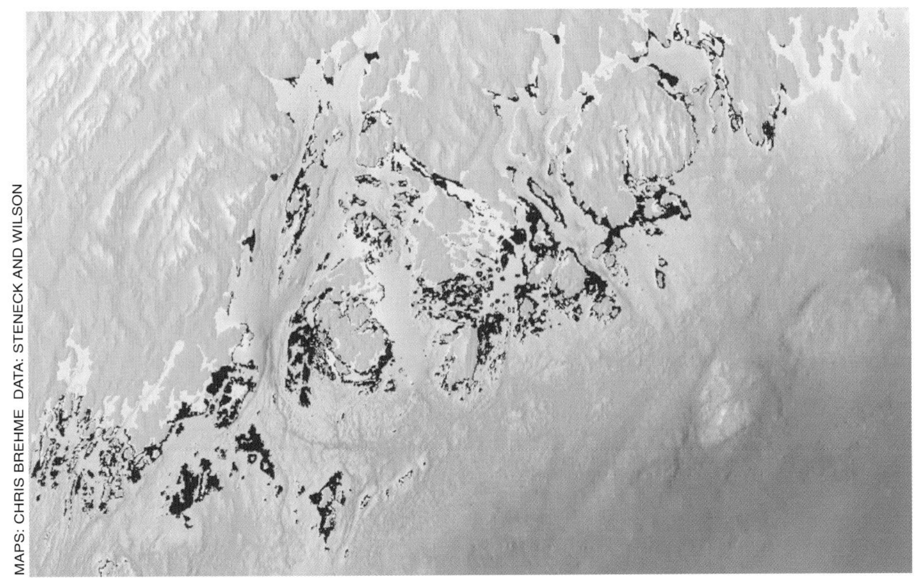

MAPS: CHRIS BREHME DATA: STENECK AND WILSON

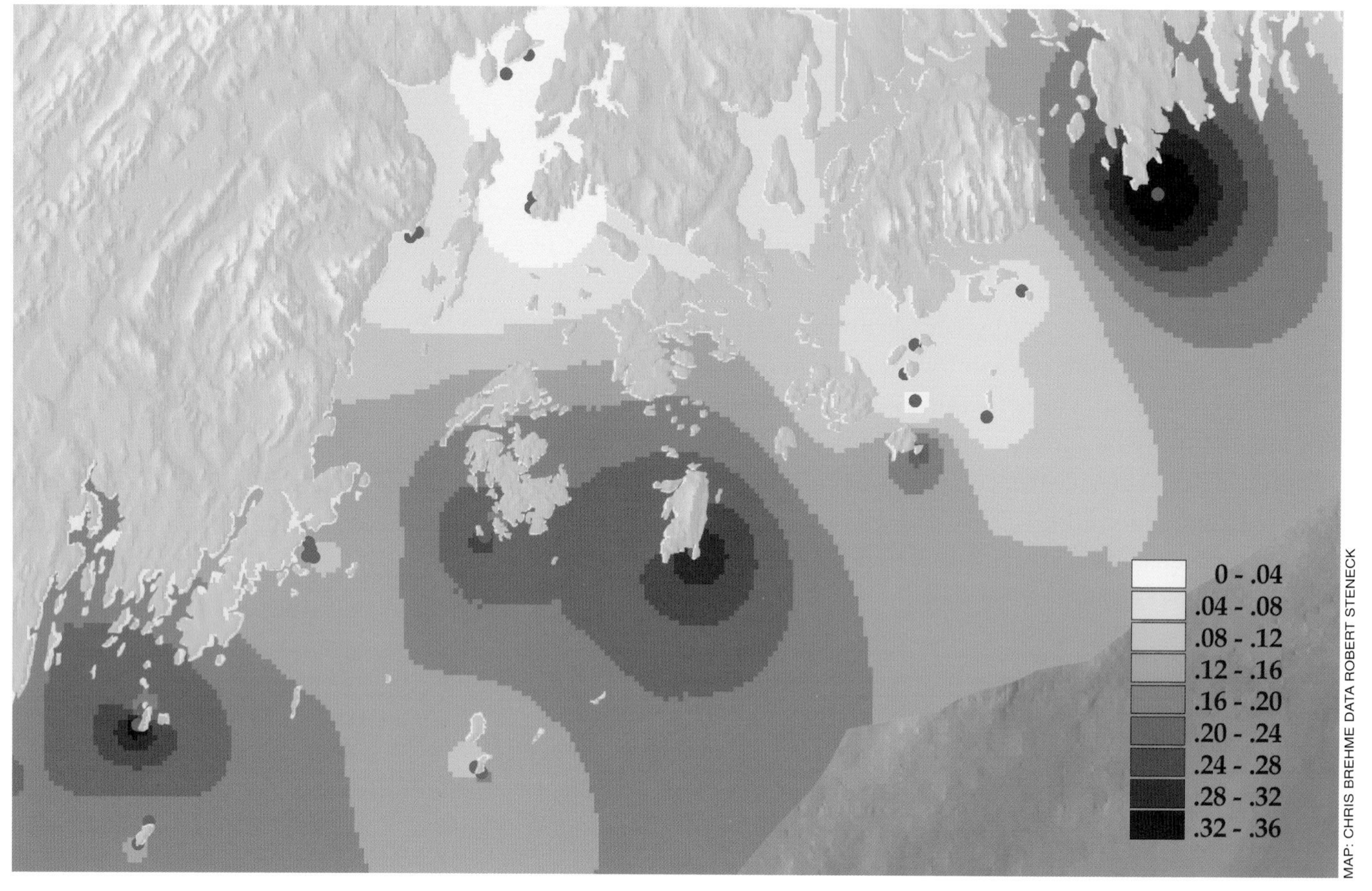

MAP: CHRIS BREHME DATA ROBERT STENECK

The distribution of young lobsters collected from underwater sampling stations along the midcoast region of Maine show a distinct pattern of 'hot spots' and 'cold spots' of abundance. (Based on the work of Bob Steneck and his colleagues for 2001)

counter-clockwise offshore, leaving post larvae in the upper (warmer) waters at the edge of this front. This front persists through the peak settlement time, which usually occurs from early August to late September.

Intertidal Sampling As part of the activity of the Penobscot Bay Collaborative, Diane Cowan and Sara Ellis of The Lobster Conservancy were invited to expand their intertidal monitoring program into Penobscot Bay. Since 1991, Cowan has conducted an intertidal lobster sampling program from a research site in Lowell's Cove, Casco Bay, on a year-round basis. This program has produced a long-term time series of observations. Its simple sampling technique can be used at any season of the year.

Cowan and Ellis recruited a large number of volunteers to monitor particular stretches of the lower intertidal zone along different shorelines in Penobscot Bay. With this volunteer network, Lobster Conservancy biologists established five intertidal lobster monitoring sites in Penobscot Bay in 1998 and added 13 more sites in 1999.

The volunteers set up transects parallel with the water's edge and sampled square-meter quadrats along alternating sides of the transect, returning to the same quadrat each month. This monitoring program took advantage of the easy, low-tide access to small lobsters in the intertidal zone, but because the previous sampling had been primarily restricted to a few sites in Casco Bay, no one really knew whether the resulting patterns could be extended to other regions.

Cowan and Ellis's intertidal results corresponded nicely with Steneck and Wilson's benthic results. The biologists and their volunteer monitors found that lobsters in the intertidal zone favor rocky habitats over eelgrass or other habitats.

More important, the results show a strong positive correlation between the densities of intertidal and subtidal lobsters in Penobscot Bay. Just as Steneck and Wilson found a consistent pattern of higher densities in the outer bay and virtually no young lobsters in the inner bay, Ellis and Cowan reported that juvenile lobsters were present at all the sampling stations of outer Penobscot Bay. Similarly, juvenile lobsters were present in the intertidal areas of western Penobscot Bay shorelines, just as they were in subtidal samples. However, juvenile lobsters were not found at any of the stations from the inner portions of Penobscot Bay. Ellis and Cowan's work is especially significant because intertidal sampling is a relatively low cost monitoring technique, as compared to subtidal sampling.

A Few Consistent Patterns In the Penobscot Bay Collaborative, data from different stages of the lobster life cycle were collected using widely differing techniques. Steneck, Wahle and Wilson used SCUBA techniques to sample the distribution of early settlers and juvenile lobsters. Cowan and Ellis used volunteers in the lower intertidal zone to sample the distribution of new settlers and juveniles. Yet the patterns that emerged—new settlers and juveniles in the outer bay, but not in the inner bay—were remarkably consistent. When different sampling regimes revealed similar patterns, scientists, trained to be skeptical about everyone's data including their own, began to get into the comfort zone - the patterns were real and not just a statistical mirage. Incidentally, the pattern of declining settlement and juvenile densities as one moves up bays and estuaries has been observed elsewhere, in the Damariscotta River and in Narragansett Bay.

Nevertheless, as noted earlier, the presence of early settlers and juveniles in the outer but not the inner bay could result from two different mechanisms. The Eastern Maine Coastal Current could deliver larvae to the mouth of the bay but not to its interior. Or the larvae from local broodstock in the bay could be cycled by local current gyres around the mid-bay islands (North Haven and Vinalhaven) and settle in the outer bay. Or the observations could result from some combination of the two hypotheses.

Intertidal sampling with Lobster Conservancy volunteers, Waterman's Beach, South Thomaston.

SHERI FLOGE

One way to sort out the relative contributions of these hypotheses is to develop a circulation model of the currents in Penobscot Bay, based on measurements from buoys, data on bottom conditions, and other inputs. More information is needed about the location of broodstock lobsters just before they release their eggs. Combining direct observations of egg releases with a computerized circulation model may allow researchers to test different scenarios to explain the patterns of newly settled lobsters that they have observed in the field.

The Value of A Settlement Index Intensive sampling of planktonic and recently settled juveniles by participants in the Penobscot Bay Collaborative during the last three years has focused not only on the spatial distribution, but also on the absolute numbers recorded by three different sampling methods—intertidal, bottom dives and surface tows. In addition to the intensive larval sampling information collected between1999 and 2001, the Collaborative has had the benefit of a much longer time series of settlement strength that Wahle of the Bigelow Laboratory has maintained since 1989 in the Boothbay region, west of Penobscot Bay. Incze has maintained planktonic larval data for the same time period.

From the accumulated results of all sampling of larval lobsters along the coast of Maine, it is apparent that larval numbers began declining in 1996 and continued declining for the next four years. Larval numbers reached their lowest ebb recorded at any time during the 12-year time series in the summer of 2000. Then in 2001, the Gulf of Maine produced a big surprise: the number of larval lobsters rebounded to one of the highest levels observed during the recent time period.

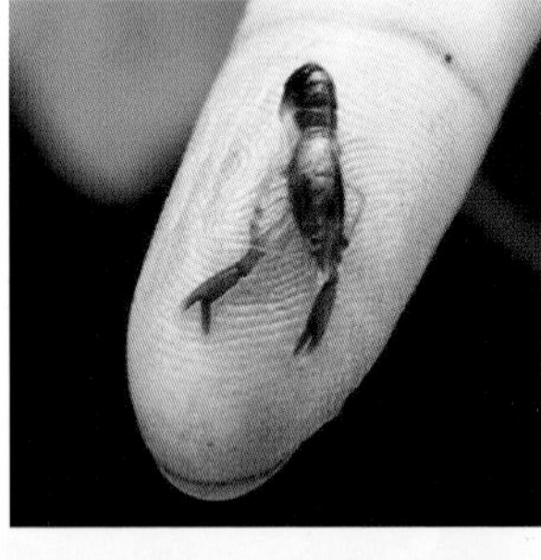

Newly settled baby lobsters collected from the intertidal zone.

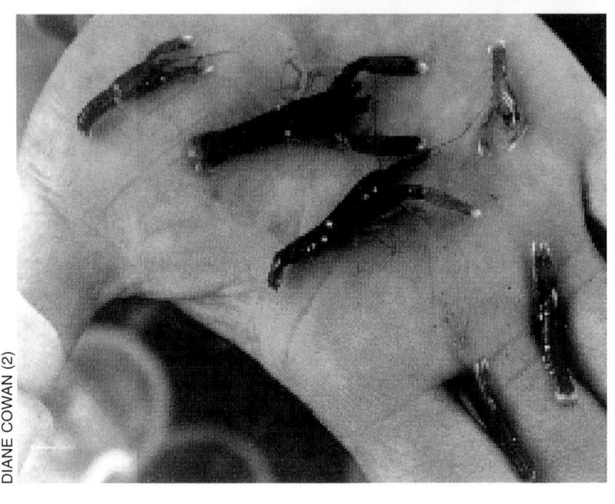

DIANE COWAN (2)

Because the correlation between late stage lobster larvae and the number of settlers on the bottom is strong, and because the linkage of settlers in an area to the number of one- and two-year-olds is also strong, a consistent five-year decline in larval lobsters is of concern. If there is a link between settlement strength and recruitment to the fishery, then the number of lobsters entering the fishery can be expected to decline in the near future. The number of lobsters that enter the fishery for harvest in 2002 and 2003 may diminish, and this decrease could last for a period of three or more years.

Members of the Collaborative are now focused on what mechanisms could explain the radically different levels of lobster larval abundance between 2000 and 2001. One idea to test is whether the larval differences between the two years are correlated with different water temperatures. There is a good deal of anecdotal evidence that unusually warm bottom temperatures occurred during the summer of 2000. More southerly species, including blue crabs and black sea bass, were both reported in the Gulf of Maine that summer. Many lobstermen reported an unusu-

Diane Cowan

INTERTIDAL SAMPLING: A POWERFUL, COST-EFFECTIVE TOOL

Lobsters have fascinated Diane Cowan since the ninth grade. She wrote a report on lobsters for class, and the very next year became SCUBA-certified so she could catch them for dinner in the waters of Long Island Sound. In college, Cowan became interested in animal behavior and communication systems. She went on to study lobster courtship behavior and the chemical signals that are involved in mating, called pheromones, for her Ph.D. dissertation at the Boston University Marine Program in Woods Hole, Massachusetts. Cowan came to Maine in 1992 and took a temporary teaching position at Bates College in Lewiston. She was kayaking with a friend in Harpswell when they noticed two boys turning over rocks at the water's edge. When Cowan asked what they were doing, the boys replied that they were looking for baby lobsters. Realizing that this would be a good opportunity for student involvement, Cowan soon brought one of her classes to the cove at low tide and had them looking under rocks too. The trip was a success, and soon Cowan developed a standard sampling method to quantify lobsters in the cove each month. In order to figure out if intertidal lobsters were unique to that area, Cowan had a student do a senior thesis project on intertidal lobsters throughout the New England coast. The student found lobsters at the low-tide mark at sites from Connecticut, on the shore of Long Island Sound, to Winter Harbor, Maine.

SARA ELLIS

Next, Cowan and the Harpswell Conservation Commission conducted a survey at sites throughout Harpswell, with the help of volunteers. From this survey, she saw the potential for a long-term monitoring program throughout the Gulf of Maine, conducted by trained volunteers using valid scientific techniques. In 1996 Cowan founded The Lobster Conservancy (TLC), and began enlisting and training an army of volunteers to perform the surveys. In 1998, TLC was asked to join the Penobscot Bay Collaborative to train and oversee volunteers all around the bay. Cowan credits The Lobster Conservancy's executive director, Sara Ellis, for spearheading the effort.

Cowan believes these surveys are a powerful, cost-effective tool for discerning trends in the lobster population. "With intertidal monitoring we are able to detect lobster settlement in space and time," she says. "We currently monitor sites from Massachusetts to Isle au Haut, and have a nine-year data set from Lowell's Cove in Harpswell."

Because the intertidal zone is the edge of the lobster's habitat, Cowan thinks it's an important area to monitor. "If there was a problem with a population," she says, "you would expect to see it first at the margin of its distribution." Beyond the value of the scientific data, Cowan also sees the monitoring program as valuable in terms of education and outreach. "It's important to involve citizens in these projects to raise awareness within a community about the value of their surroundings." (BN)

Institute intertidal sampler Sheri Floge, measuring a juvenile lobster. (right) Battling lobster defending territory

ally early molt of lobsters that year, presumably as a result of warmer bottom temperatures early in the season. Summer bottom temperatures may be a function of the winter surface temperatures of water on the Scotian Shelf that enters the eastern Gulf of Maine, or of deeper waters entering through the Northeast Channel between Georges and Brown's Banks. During the 2001 summer season, water temperatures appear to have been cooler in the eastern Gulf of Maine, and there were fewer storms, so southwesterly winds might have delivered more larvae to coastal locations. Whichever mechanism - or another yet to be understood - explains the dynamics of larval abundance, it is certain that the federal investment GOMOOS (the Gulf of Maine Ocean Observing System, the nation's first system of coastal buoys, radar and satellite downloading facilities) will help provide an answer.

Larval Tows and Light Traps Monitoring larval lobster numbers from a boat towing a specialized net at a constant speed at an appropriate location in coastal currents is an expensive and elaborate undertaking. In other parts of the world, notably in Australia and New Zealand, managers and fishermen have developed larval lobster collectors that have produced numbers reliable enough for management purposes.

A scientist from the Maine Department of Marine Resources, Jay Krouse, first demonstrated that the larvae of American lobsters are attracted to light. Krouse deployed light traps in the inner and outer harbor at Boothbay, and was able to catch a significant number of lobster larvae.

In the 2001 field season, Bob Steneck and an assistant designed and built a number of larval light traps. Corrie Roberts of the Island Institute deployed the traps for Steneck at four different sites in the waters of Isle au Haut, Criehaven, Monhegan and Allen Island. More work remains to be done to determine whether these traps, or a combination of other methods produce estimates of larval lobsters numbers that correlate with future harvests. The answer to this question has large implications for future management.

NICK CALOYIANIS

PETER RALSTON

6

The Life of Young Lobsters

RECRUITMENT AND MIGRATION

How and where do lobsters move along the coast and into the bays of Maine? Do they stay in one place or migrate long distances throughout the Gulf of Maine.? Rick Wahle of the Bigelow Laboratory, an Island fellow and a group of cooperating lobster fishermen from Vinalhaven teamed up in an effort to find the answers to these questions by tagging tens of thousands of lobsters.

LOBSTERMEN COMPLAIN THAT BIOLOGISTS who predict a decline in harvests from too much fishing are ignoring a compelling piece of evidence: the high number of juvenile lobsters fishermen find in their traps. But a lobsterman's traps are not, in fact, designed as a scientific tool to estimate the abundance of lobsters, especially juveniles. They are designed to catch lobsters in the restricted range of legal sizes.

The patterns of young settlers that Bob Steneck detected and described as "hot spots" of abundance in Penobscot Bay also extend to patterns of juveniles that appear in nearby quadrat samples, as well as from lobsterman's traps that fish in the same area. And Diane Cowan's lobster sampling in the intertidal zone shows similar patterns.

From previous work, Rick Wahle of the Bigelow Laboratory has helped provide lobster biologists with a deeper understanding of linkages during the early phases of a lobster's life cycle, especially between the "settlement" stage and later juvenile stages. Through suction sampling, Wahle has shown a strong correlation between the number of settlers on the bottom and the number of two- and three-year-old lobsters in research plots. This important finding suggests that after young lobsters reach sheltered living spaces on the bottom, their mortality during the first three years of their life is quite low.

But does this relationship between settlement and the early adolescent phases of juvenile lobsters actually hold up until lobsters enter the fishery, between the ages of six and seven here on the coast of Maine? Diane Cowan has tagged lobsters in the intertidal zone and recaptured some of these lobsters up to four

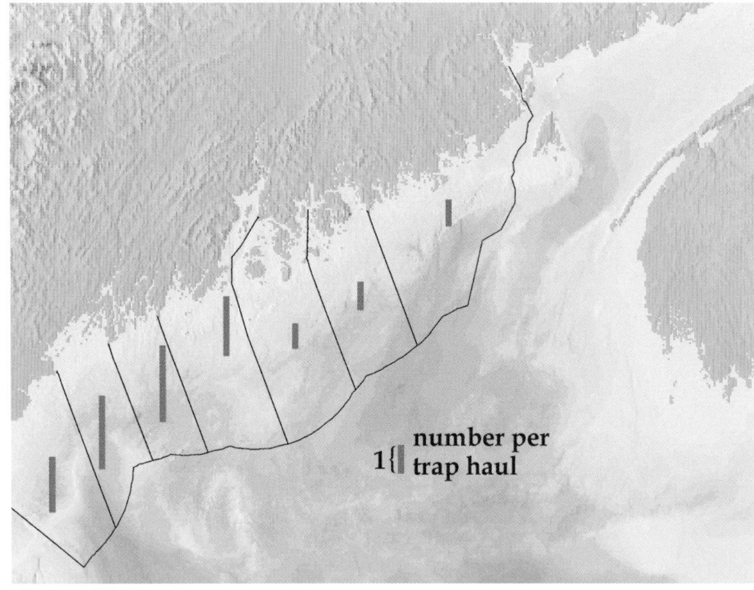

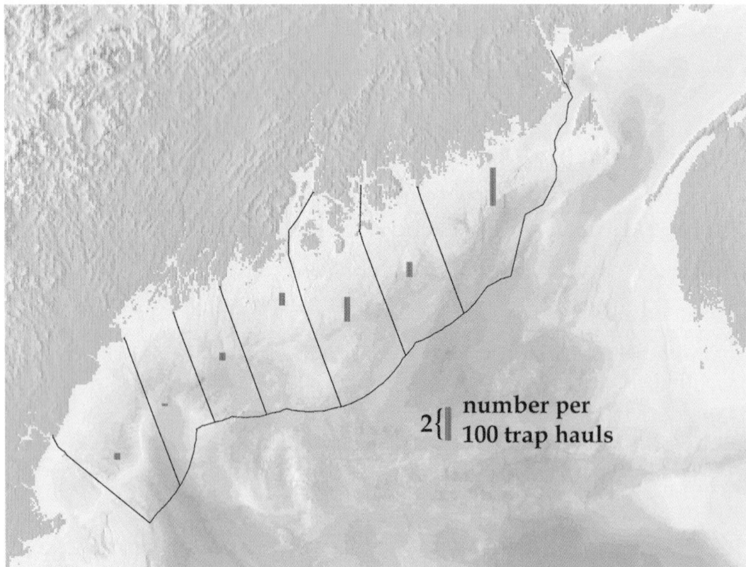

years later indicating the use of their nursery habitat for the first four to five years of benthic life. But this evidence is fragmentary. The Department of Marine Resources has now completed four years of intensive sampling, including a record of the number of juveniles that lobstermen catch in their traps. Although not yet a long term data set, the results from the sea sampling surveys between 1998 and 2000 show a pattern of juvenile abundance consistent with the patterns of larval distribution in the water column and the patterns of recent settlers to the bottom. That is, just as there are more larvae in the water column west of Penobscot Bay and also more settlers there on the bottom, there are also many more juvenile lobsters in western sections of the Maine coast than there are in eastern sections. On average, over twice as many juveniles were recorded in DMR's sea sampling survey in lobstermen's traps west of Penobscot Bay, compared to the number of juveniles found in traps to the east of Penobscot Bay.

The DMR sea sampling data, based on recording the locations of over 150,000 juvenile lobsters during the three-year period, is the most extensive data set yet compiled on the distribution of juvenile lobsters. Such data, like much of the data that are accumulating from a variety of scientific investigations, indicate that the mechanisms controlling lobster abundance are significantly different between eastern and western sections of the coast. Furthermore, this apparently fundamental shift in the patterns of lobster distribution occurs in the region of Penobscot Bay.

Although the abundance of juvenile lobsters in western sections indicates that harvests for the next several years should remain healthy there, lobster biologists still need to understand the underlying mechanisms that explain the patterns of distribution observed both in the fishery and in scientific investigations. Furthermore, biologists don't really understand how the number of juveniles in a given area relates to future harvests. Since lobsters shed their shells regularly, researchers don't really know the age of the juveniles. It is not possible to determine the age of an individual lobster the way one can learn the age of a fish.

Do juvenile lobsters between four and six years old grow at sufficiently different rates and/or migrate away from the area where they settle, masking any relationship between settlement and the time when lobsters grow large enough to be legally harvested? In other words, are the patterns lobstermen see in their traps correlated with the abundance and distribution of the size range of lobsters on the bottom? Such information will be important for stock assessment models that may one day predict future harvests. Fishermen's observations of the number of lobsters of all sizes, including juveniles in an area, need to be rigorously quantified and analyzed to determine whether they can become useful indicators.

Seasonal Movements Lobstermen have long understood the fundamental seasonal movement of lobsters along the Maine coast. In the spring and early summer, lobsters move toward the shores — along most of the Maine coast, this means lobsters move into shallower bays where water temperatures are warmer. In the late summer and fall, lobsters reverse this pattern as they move into deeper waters to spend the winter.

But do those lobsters then return to the same bays as the previous year or do they go off to other areas? In other words, do juvenile or adult lobsters have restricted "home ranges" where they live out their lives, or do they migrate from area to area along the coast in some predictable or unpredictable pattern?

The best way to address these questions is through "mark-and-recapture" projects where individual lobsters are tagged in particular locations and then recaptured, perhaps, in lobstermen's traps so their locations can be

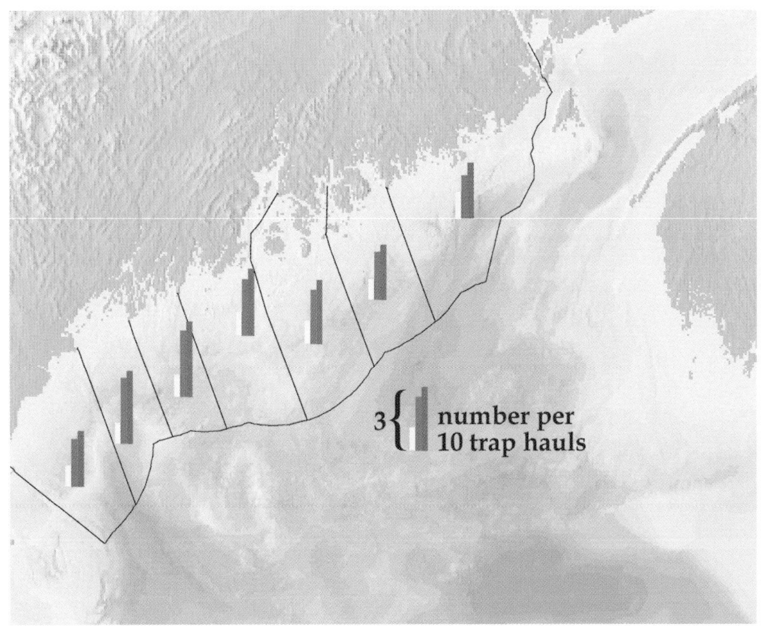

The DMR's sea sampling database now contains the records of hundreds of thousands of lobsters measured between 1998-2000. When mapped by lobster management zones , some striking patterns emerge. First, egg bearing females are reasonably uniformly distributed along the entire coast (above). However, there is a dramatic increase in number of juveniles (sublegals)sampled between 1998-2000 in zones west of Penobscot Bay over zones in eastern Maine (bottom left facing page). Furthermore, the number of large, oversized lobsters appears to be much higher in eastern Maine zones than in western zones (facing page, bottom).

reported. Wahle piloted such a tag-and-recapture effort during the winter of 2000 with Island Fellow Jessica Stevens on Monhegan Island.

The Problem of Bias Simply looking at lobster abundance based on the numbers and size distribution of lobsters in a trap may provide biased results. For example, lobsters are less likely to enter traps just before and after molting. They respond differently to different lobster baits, different trap design, and to the presence or absence of other lobsters and crabs in a trap and to differences in water temperature. In the summer of 2001, with the support of the Maine Sea Grant Program, Rick Wahle expanded his mark-and-recapture tagging project into Penobscot Bay, to test whether the estimates of abundance from mark-and-recapture correlates with the number of lobsters that divers find on the bottom.

The method Wahle used may be used as a "corrective lens" allowing a researcher to estimate the actual number of lobsters on the bottom without using labor intensive and expensive methods that rely on divers. It also allows him to estimate something that diver censuses cannot — that is, gains and losses to the local population, called "population turnover."

Researchers also want to learn what proportion of the juvenile lobsters caught in an area stay there, versus those that emigrate out of the region. Wahle's project, which is expected to extend through 2003, involves a group of lobstermen on Vinalhaven, including Walter Day, Bobby Warren and Eric Davis, who are participating in the Department of Marine Resources' sea sampling program. The project has received additional support from the Island Institute Fellow Nate Geraldi, and

PETER RALSTON

Island fellow, Nate Geraldi at work on tag recapture project off Vinalhaven.

Walter Day of Vinalhaven

"NOW WE ARE ALL LOOKING FOR THE ANSWERS"

PETER RALSTON

Walter Day of Vinalhaven has been fishing for lobsters in Penobscot Bay since he was 10 years old. Like his father before him and now his oldest son, Jason, he has made a good living from the sea by knowing where and when the lobsters will be crawling amongst the coves and offshore ledges of his home island. Nevertheless, in the course of participating in the research of the Penobscot Bay Collaborative, he says he, too, learned some things about his home waters.

"It was a learning experience from both ends," he says, "and I think now we have stopped just looking at the scientists and talking about how wrong they are, and I think they also have a new respect for the knowledge of fishermen, and now we are all just looking for the answers." He cites what he has learned about the geologic structure of the deep underwater areas off the island. "I even found out some things I never knew I was missing," he says, and points out that it was the same for the researchers, who seemed often to raise yet another question for each one answered.

In his years of chasing both lobsters and herring, Day has seen the ebb and flood of various species, and knows intimately the effects such fluctuations can have on him and the couple of hundred other lobstermen on Vinalhaven, which supports one of the largest lobster fleets of any town in Maine — and certainly the largest of any island. In connection with the Penobscot Bay Project, he took out dozens of sea-samplers on his boat, and gladly accepted integrating them into his workday. Thousands of individual lobsters have been measured on his boat, providing information that feeds an ever-growing database. Lobsters by the millions have been taken by generations of commercial lobstermen from these waters, and Day hopes that with newfound knowledge driving its judicious management, that this resource will last forever. Now that he has become personally more involved in research projects, Day says, "the hook is set and I want to keep on working together with the scientists, puzzling out the workings of the bay." And so he has, this past year donating some of his own traps and time for a tagging study. He continues to carry on both research and fishing, working day in and day out on the water, hoping to wrest not only a living but also a deeper understanding of the waters themselves. (BN)

from the Institute's Corrie Roberts, skipper of the research vessel ALICE SIEGMUND, which has been used to support the project.

Wahle, Roberts and Geraldi marked an area of a square kilometer off the southwestern shores of Vinalhaven. This area, just south of Vinalhaven's Carver's Harbor, is a major lobster producing area in Penobscot Bay. At peak season, the study area is saturated with over 1,000 other traps of commercial fishermen. The researchers placed 64 traps that had been modified by removing their escape vents. They then marked all the lobsters they caught, including the juveniles, with streamer tags and a toll-free telephone number, and asked lobstermen to phone in the location of where these individuals were recaptured. These reports would provide information on how much lobsters move around.

The project got underway in 2001. During the first field season, Wahle and his crew marked over 11,000 juvenile lobsters on this small piece of bottom. During the first few months of the project, the team received over 250 calls from fishermen in the area, reporting recapture information. Another several thousand lobsters were recaptured in the research traps.

This research project continued through the 2002 field season, and will extend through 2003. Preliminary results show that the abundance from the non-vented research traps was similar to the "ground truth" observations: from 25,000 to 50,000 lobsters within the area, depending on the time of season.

At the end of the project, the team hopes to have pioneered a new method

PETER RALSTON

Tagging a lobster with a bright yellow, bar-coded tag before returning it to the water.

Rick Wahle

DEVELOPING AN EARLY WARNING SYSTEM

A research scientist at Bigelow Laboratory since 1995, Dr. Rick Wahle has studied the ecology and fisheries of a number of invertebrates, but he has probably invested most of his sweat and blood in the American lobster. For over 15 years, he has been studying the oceanographic and ecological processes affecting American lobster populations with an eye toward using that information in the development of an early warning system for trends in the harvest.

PETER RALSTON

As a Ph.D. student at the University of Maine in the late 1980s, Wahle applied a new sampling methodology to the problem of counting lobsters at the earliest stages of their bottom-dwelling existence, when they hide cryptically in crevices among rocks along the coast. The underwater suction sampling application he developed opened a window on a segment of the lobster life cycle that had long eluded science. By this method during the 1990s, Wahle and collaborators Lew Incze and Bob Steneck, among others, evaluated linkages between larval supply and settlement strength; and then, the link between settlement strength and survival into later years.

Adopting these methods, the states of Maine, Massachusetts and Rhode Island now track lobster settlement along much of New England's coast with the aim of determining whether year-to-year differences in settlement will be as useful in forecasting New England's lobster landings as it is in lobster fisheries in other parts of the world. Because it takes five to nine years for a lobster to mature to the fishery, it will still be several years before we know how accurately any settlement index will predict harvests. Nonetheless, the scientific findings and collaborations forged in the process set the stage for the lobster emphasis of the Penobscot Bay project.

The fact that annual swings in larval settlement in Maine and Rhode Island are consistent suggest that oceanic or climatic factors affecting larval supply operate at a scale much larger than the Gulf of Maine. This has spawned a collaboration with Andrew Thomas of the University of Maine's Remote Sensing Lab to assess correlations of sea surface temperature in New England's offshore waters with settlement strength nearshore. While diver-based methods continue to contribute a great deal to our understanding of lobster ecology, as lobsters move away from shallow nurseries they often move beyond the safe and practical limits of diving. That is where traps become the most practical alternative. In his most recent work, Wahle has brought together the unlikely combination of fishing industry expertise with mark-recapture methods developed for small mammals. These techniques may provide new insights into whether lobster traps can become a more accurate tool in obtaining direct estimates of lobster abundance.

(BN)

TRAP BY TRAP,
A RESEARCHER AND FISHERMEN BUILD A RELATIONSHIP

By Jessica Stevens

Based upon a year of experience conducting lobster research in cooperation with lobstermen from York to Jonesport, I thought that I might need a hook. So I stayed up late baking oatmeal cookies. After all, I was going to be asking for much help. I never suspected that a small fleet of lobstermen ten miles offshore of the coast might by nature be more cooperative than could be obtained with a bribe of a million cookies, cakes and pies.

PETER RALSTON

Between March and May 2000, the Monhegan lobster fishing fleet participated in a pilot study focused on tagging and tracking sublegal lobsters, as well as assisting with the collection of baseline catch and effort data. This is a collaborative effort of the Island Institute, Dr. Rick Wahle of the Bigelow Laboratory for Ocean Sciences, lobster biologist Carl Wilson at the state Department of Marine Resources (DMR), the Monhegan community and myself, Monhegan's first Island Fellow. Through the Island Institute's new Fellowship Program I took up residence on Monhegan in March to work with the lobstermen as well as assist in the school. I was charged with locating a site for tagging, and then tagging as many sublegal lobsters as possible. Multiple schedules had to be taken into account. In a given day, I might get aboard four different lobster boats that must haul within the same 0.7 nautical mile square box at different times. For statistical reasons, lobsters had to be caught and released in very specific areas. Taking the weather into consideration as well, the complexity of the project started to become clear. All of this work would have remained on paper if it were not for the efforts of the Monhegan lobstermen.

To begin with, the Monhegan fishermen took a risk. A pilot study is the first stage in a scientific study, more often providing information on how to make a study work than providing conclusive data. Monhegan lobstermen each agreed to close the vents on a small number of traps. For a fisherman, potentially sacrificing the fishing ability of traps is a noteworthy step.

These lobstermen gave me their time also. The welcoming nature of Shermie Stanley and his fishhouse made it possible to call an informal introductory meeting when I arrived on the island. The Monhegan fishermen proved themselves incredibly flexible on short notice, at times waiting to haul in the tagging area until I had completed work aboard another boat or finished teaching a lesson on lobsters at the island school.

They took the extra time necessary to head into the lee of the island so that I could shift from boat to boat safely. They provided extra bins, baskets and banders at my request. Thanks to this collaboration, close to 1,000 sublegal lobsters were tagged. In addition, well over 5,000 lobsters were measured, providing supplementary information about catch and effort that will be related to the population of sublegal lobsters studied. A refined method was established and problems worked out. What does it take to get a group of lobstermen to show such active participation in fisheries science? To its credit, the Monhegan fleet is a conservation-minded group to begin with. But being a resident scientist was important here too. I was available round-the-clock to organize logistics, ask questions, answer questions, be accountable. I was there not only to observe, but also to be a part of a day's fishing from start to finish. This overlap made communication between the harvester and the scientist a two-way avenue, a road as well traveled as the stretch of water home to the Monhegan fleet. I applaud and thank the Monhegan fishermen and the Monhegan community for welcoming a scientist into their space. They demonstrated a level of participation in science well above that which can be coaxed from a fisherman with an oatmeal raisin cookie.

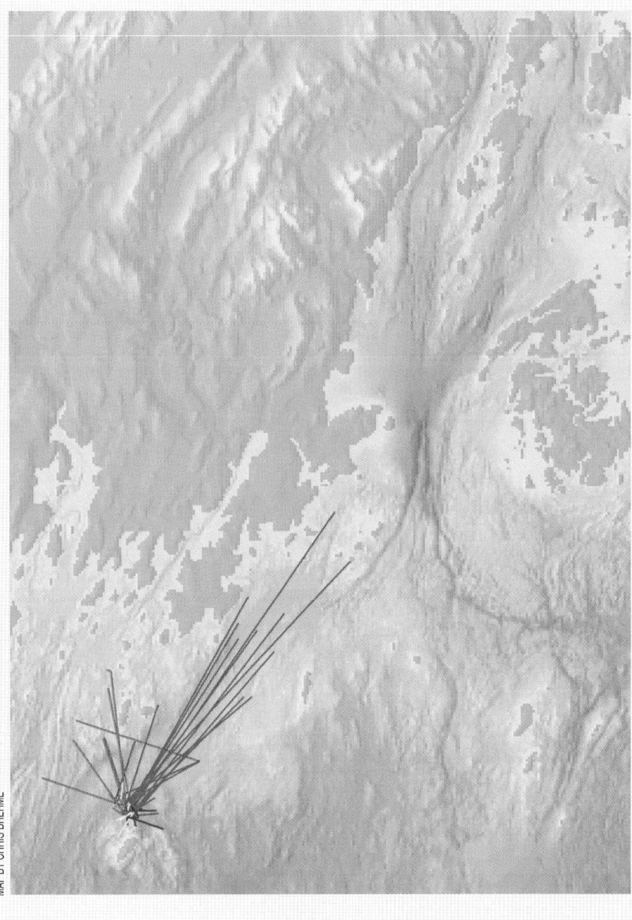
MAP BY CHRIS BREHME

(From "*The Working Waterfront,*" July, 2000)

(Map):*Lobsters tagged in the winter around Monhegan move shoreward in spring into nearby Muscongus and Penosbcot Bays.*

demonstrating the use of these "ventless" traps and the cooperation of local lobstermen to develop a new, cost-effective stock assessment method. Incidentally, the long distance migration record, recorded on the telephone voice recorder, was from a Wal-Mart store in Wisconsin — where someone had apparently purchased a tagged lobster!

NICK CALOYIANIS

Female lobsters on excavated 'nest' cavities off Grand Manan Island.

PETER RALSTON

7

Old Hands, New Technology

NEW TOOLS TACKLE OLD QUESTIONS

A mix of traditional techniques and new tools are beginning to be employed to monitor the status and health of Maine's lobster resource. Some of the tools have been developed by lobstermen themselves and are widely employed, others are new high tech methods that are slowly gaining acceptance in an industry that is well known for its skepticism of 'new and improved methods.'

ON DEC. 11, 1933, MAINE SEA and Shore Fisheries Commissioner Horatio Crie briefed the Maine Legislature on his proposal for dealing with disastrously poor catches in the state's lobster fishery. His plan involved a new tool: a "double gauge" that would protect juveniles and older "broodstock" lobsters. The Legislature adopted Crie's plan the following spring, and since then every lobster fisherman in Maine has been required to carry a brass gauge for measuring his catch.

Today this familiar tool is at the heart of lobster conservation in Maine. But it is only one of many tools, some of which make the lobsterman more efficient, while others provide an ever-growing body of information critical to understanding and managing the lobster resource.

Inside a boat's wheelhouse, for example, one will find banks of computer screens that relay information on depth, position, course, and location of potential obstacles. The global positioning system (GPS) allows a fisherman to locate himself more precisely in the water or over particular parts of the sea bottom. Sonar systems, developed by the Navy to navigate the deep seas or hunt foreign submarines, have been adapted to map the once opaque expanses of the bottom, and may be further modified to be able to estimate the number of different kinds of marine creatures. Remotely operated vehicles and small submersibles allow access to the realm of the lobster itself—one can begin, for the first time, to see how lobsters develop from one life stage to another.

Geographic Informations Systems (GIS) Until recently, there has been a chasm of miscommunication between fishermen and scientists viewing the same resource. Many fisheries scientists have viewed fishermen as short-sighted individuals unable to avoid the tragedy of the commons. Many fishermen, meanwhile, have tended to view marine scientists as theorists who don't go out on boats much and therefore are out of touch with the ever-changing marine environment.

The Penobscot Bay Collaborative has endeavored to present as much scientific information as possible in geographic formats, rather than solely in tables, charts and graphs of numbers. Fishermen depend on highly specific, place-based knowledge of the marine environment, and the managers of the Collaborative have believed that geographically presented information will enable fishermen to test scientific information against their own observation and experience.

For example, if scientists present their information on currents, temperatures, habitats and population trends as highly accurate but abstract sets of numbers, fishermen may tune them out. If this same information is portrayed geographically, however, there is potential for discussion, if not agreement. Even when scientific information doesn't correspond with fishermen's observations, geographic information is inherently more inclusive—it is, in short, in the language everyone can understand.

COURTESY BOB STENECK

Lobstermen and lobster scientists who participated in submarine research dives aboard the Johnson 'Sea Link' to survey the distribution of lobster brood stock in 1996.

NICK CALOYIANIS

Linda Mercer

"The Pen Bay Collaborative is ahead of its time."

Linda Mercer first became interested in fisheries science during her senior year in college. She was working as an intern with an ichthyologist at the Smithsonian Institution in Washington, D.C.

"I spent a month dissecting tuna and by the end of the internship, I was hooked!" Mercer enrolled in an ichthyology course the summer after college, and went on to work for the Massachusetts Division of Marine Fisheries (DMF). She attended graduate school at the Virginia Institute of Marine Science, and did her dissertation research on the reproductive biology and population dynamics of black sea bass.

Mercer was first exposed to the politics of fisheries management in North Carolina, where she worked as a fisheries biologist writing fishery management plans for a variety of species. In 1995, Mercer became the director of the Bureau of Resource Management at the Maine Department of Marine Resources (DMR), a position she still holds. As director, she oversees the bureau's many research, monitoring and education programs, as well as identifying and planning new programs as needs arise.

During the planning stages of the Penobscot Bay Collaborative, Mercer submitted ideas for collaborative research on behalf of the Maine DMR, including a larval fish and a cod habitat study. When the project's focus was narrowed to lobster research, Mercer helped to identify some of the important questions regarding lobsters in Penobscot Bay.

PETER RALSTON

She supports the type of collaborative research that took place during the project. "The Pen Bay project was ahead of its time in terms of getting fishermen and scientists to sit down and talk." To that end, Mercer convened a series of meetings in May of 2000 in which fishermen, scientists and fisheries managers got together and discussed research priorities for the major commercial fisheries in Maine.

"Maine has become a national leader in both working collaboratively with fishermen, and sharing management responsibility," says Mercer. Encouraged by Mercer and other state scientists and managers, Maine has been working closely with the lobster zone councils on management issues. Still, she sees a need to do more. "There is not a strong role for zone councils in identifying areas of future research," she says. "We need to work more closely with the councils and improve the exchange of information on research and monitoring programs."

(BN)

Unloading lobsters, Scribners Monthly, June, 1881.

Linda Mercer, the head of Maine's Department of Marine Resources research division, understands the need for better means of presenting scientific findings to the fishing community. Mercer recognized that the Penobscot Bay Collaborative could be the catalyst to test the broader use of geographically presented information, especially if maps displaying scientific information could be posted on the Department's web site. Over a two-year period, the Collaborative invested a substantial amount of funding at DMR to help the agency upgrade its GIS capacity with new hardware, software and training.

In 2001 Carl Wilson and his colleagues at DMR were able to post the complete set of the state's sea sampling database on the web for the first time. Sea sampling data are reported both in geographic and tabular formats, allowing users to select the dates of interest. The results are reported either by county or by lobster zone. (Maine's lobster zones are geographic divisions of the coast into seven different areas in which each area is managed by local committees. elected by the lobstermen themselves.)

The experience of the Collaborative to date is that the way information on a particular fisheries resource such as lobsters is presented can have a large effect on how it is received.

Global Positioning System (GPS) Neal Pettigrew used "drifters" to test his hypotheses regarding currents in the bay. A signaling device attached to each drifter was tracked by a communications satellite using the Global Positioning System (GPS). Unlike the other satellites previously described, which orbit the earth, this satellite is in a fixed position, stationed over our bit of the earth. It recorded the position of Pettigrew's drifters several times a day and forwarded the information daily to his lab. Reading the output, Pettigrew could follow the track of the drifters and determine if they had stopped moving, needed to be freed from lobster gear, or had circumnavigated the mid-bay islands.

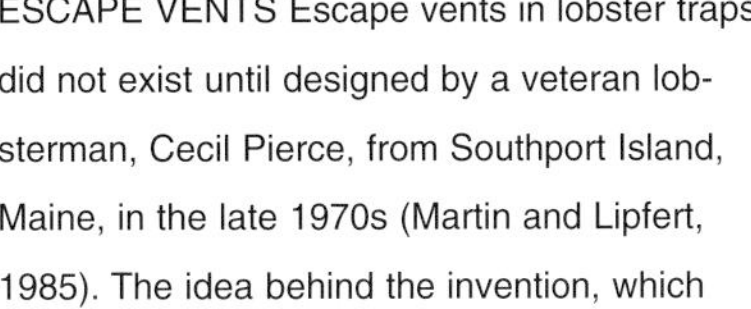

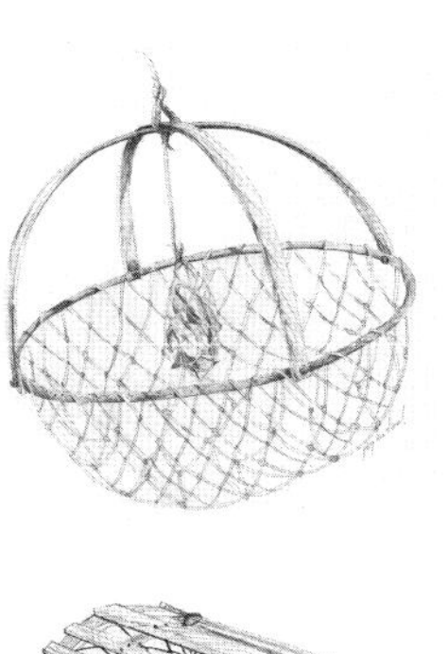

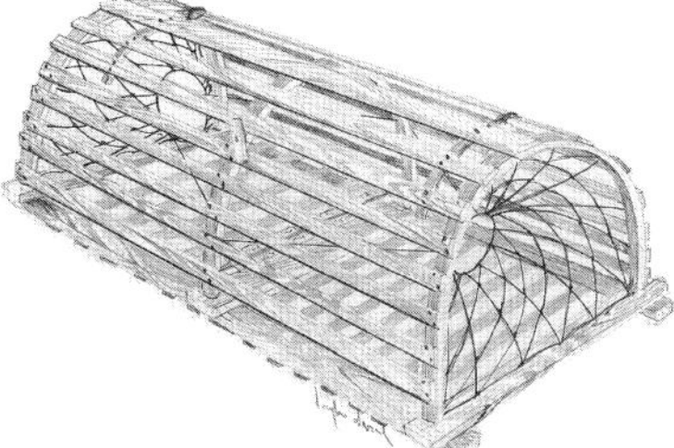

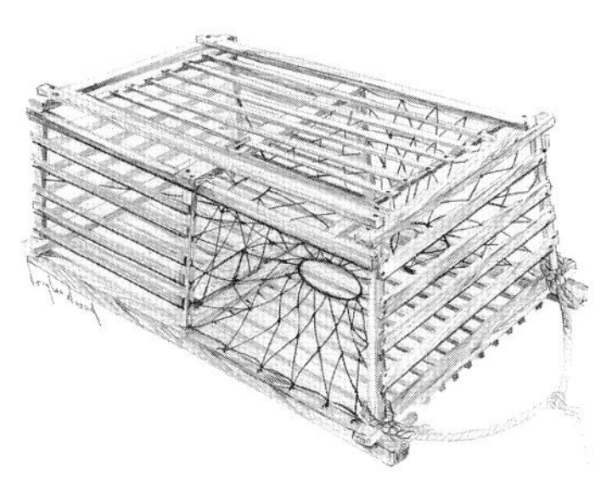

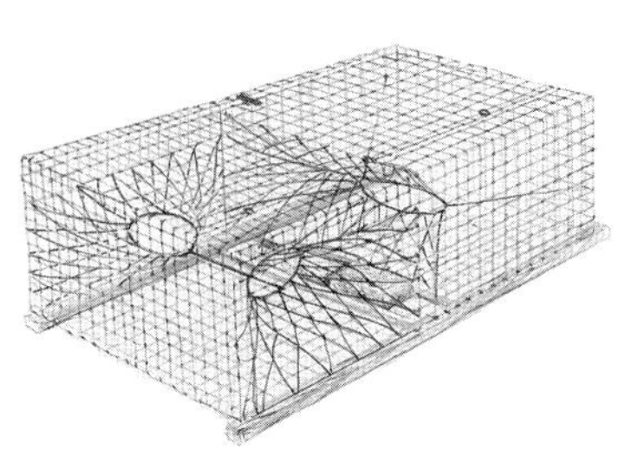

DRAWINGS: DOUG. ALVORD, COURTESY MAINE MARITIME MUSEUM

Evolution of the design of the Maine lobster trap from 1850s (top) to the rounded trap (1880s-1960s) to the square parlor trap of the mid-Twentieth century to the wire trap which became established in the 1980s.

ESCAPE VENTS Escape vents in lobster traps did not exist until designed by a veteran lobsterman, Cecil Pierce, from Southport Island, Maine, in the late 1970s (Martin and Lipfert, 1985). The idea behind the invention, which Pierce declined to patent but instead donated to the industry, is allow undersized juvenile lobsters to escape from the trap while retaining the legal sized lobsters. When vents are removed or plugged, juveniles are retained.

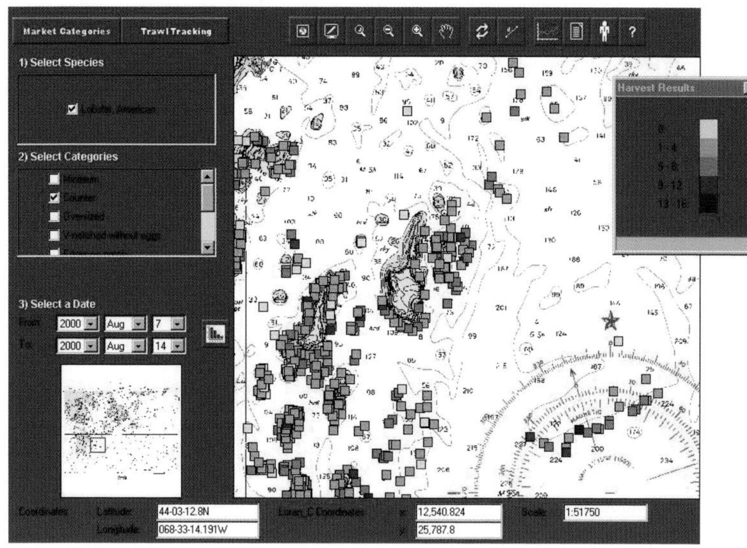

Electronic logbook data records the location of harvested lobsters for individual lobstermen, producing a complete record of how much they caught and precisely where and when. Courtesy of Thistle Marine, LLC.

"Dependent" vs. "Independent" Other new tools serving a conservation purpose include the "electronic logbook," which allows fishermen to analyze the success of different fishing strategies and provide up-to-date information to the state for stock assessments.

Information collected and organized in the electronic logbook isn't as detailed as what's gathered through the use of yet another tool, sea sampling. A sea sampler typically analyzes a portion of a fisherman's haul, recording information about size, sex, whether V-notched, depth, location and other parameters as the catch comes aboard.

Such data reflect only the portion of the lobster population that is "trappable." In fisheries science parlance, this data is "fisheries dependent" because it is limited to those areas where fishermen operate and to those lobsters willing to enter a trap. Since fishermen tend to fish where there are lobsters, it can overestimate lobster abundance if extrapolated to the entire bottom.

Sampling that is "fisheries independent" is usually conducted by scientists and interns using scuba gear for vacuum sampling and visual surveys. While this kind of sampling can also include trawl surveys, ROV surveys and ventless trap surveys and can provide very detailed and accurate data, it is often expensive and covers relatively small areas.

A New Generation One tool, still under development, may be one of the most significant products of the Penobscot Bay Project: a model of the bay's circulation. Modern computing has allowed the development of models based on millions of bits of data, models that include the three physical dimensions as well as the dimension of time. The weather report on the evening news is based on models of climatic and atmospheric activity.

Built of numbers, computer-based numerical models describe the complex web of interactions among parts of a system - in our case, the currents circulating within

Huijie Xue

LINKING PHYSICS AND BIOLOGY

Huijie Xue, Associate Professor in the School of Marine Sciences at the University of Maine, is a graduate of the Shandong College of Oceanology, in Qingdao, China. She earned a Ph.D. in Atmospheric and Ocean Sciences from Princeton University. Her research interests include understanding and describing the movement of ocean currents and their interaction with atmospheric events. Much of her research has focused on the Gulf Stream, including the reaction of this distinctive oceanographic feature to cold air outbreaks and the creation of large meanders.

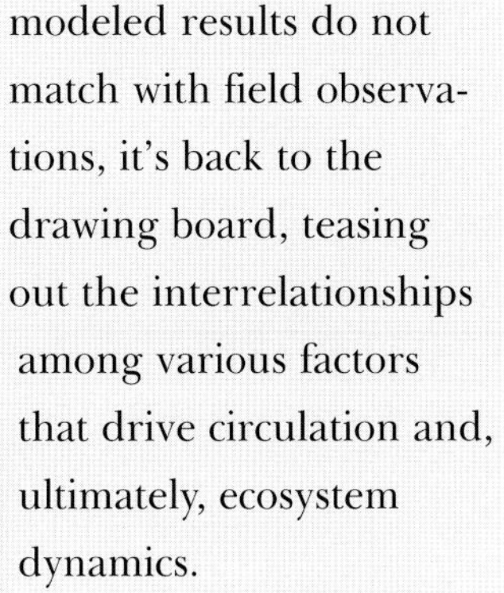

NAKOMIS NELSON

For the Penobscot Bay Collaborative, Xue has the difficult job of using numbers to capture the mysteries of the bay's circulation. By incorporating the findings of fellow members of the Collaborative, Xue captures the latest in assumptions about the movement of water in and about the bay. Numerical modeling is not a trivial task — millions of data points must be incorporated and then connected with formulas that create a dynamic whole from a series of static parts. Xue has built complex computer arrays to facilitate testing the model but it still takes several hours to complete a single run of the model. If the modeled results do not match with field observations, it's back to the drawing board, teasing out the interrelationships among various factors that drive circulation and, ultimately, ecosystem dynamics.

Xue's work is a bridge between highly theoretical notions of the behavior of the ocean and real world observations of what is actually happening. "I appreciate the opportunity to work with field researchers," says Xue, "their data provides key building blocks for my model; perhaps more importantly, their focus puts the model to use in helping to solve issues in coastal management." From theory to application, Xue is providing the link between physics and biology and between basic research and practical guidance for the resource managers and fishermen who are working together to protect a vitally important lobster fishery.

(AH)

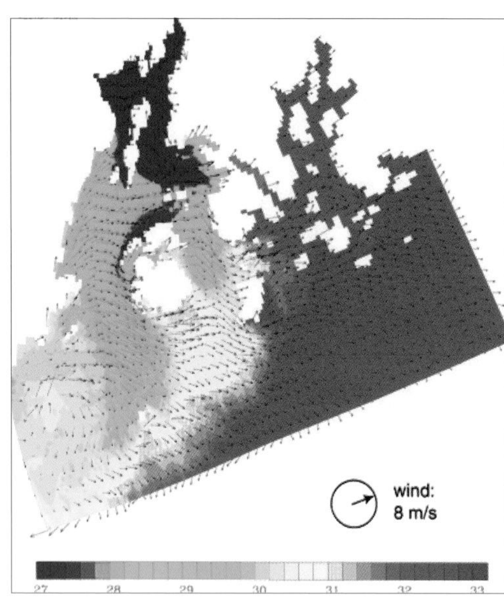

Xue's circulation model output showing surface salinity during typical high run-off conditions in April.

Penobscot Bay. Like other tools beginning with the double gauge, computer models can have profound effects on the state of Penobscot Bay's lobster resource.

Huijie Xue, professor of oceanography at the University of Maine, is using hydrographic data collected by other project scientists as well as regional weather data to craft a computer program that simulates the movement of water within the bay and identifies such properties as temperature and salinity. She began by dividing the waters of the bay and the near reaches of the Gulf of Maine into a grid of points 151 points long in the east-west dimension and 121 points high in the north-south dimension. From the surface, the grid extends downward as many as 15 points to the bottom.

The bathymetry of the bay is one of the "boundary conditions" that modelers must define. Other boundary conditions for the Penobscot Bay model include freshwater inflows from the Penobscot River, local winds, currents in the Gulf of Maine, and solar radiation. With these defined, Xue assigned data to each of the points in her grid, representing the building blocks of physical oceanography: temperature, salinity, and current speed and direction. Data are assigned to each point for each of several dates. These static points are then connected by equations that describe the relationship between a point and every other point with which it is connected. For example, how do the salinity measurements collected at ten meters below the surface by the CTD on the west bay buoy change from day to day? How does the salinity here change in relation to the salinity at ten meters a quarter-mile to the north? This mind-boggling patchwork of interrelated data is the backbone of the model.

Xue has continued to refine her calculations, testing different configurations to see how they affect the model's output. This is no trivial task - each run of the model takes several hours of computer time, even on Xue's bank of powerful processors. The output from the model is not easily viewed in a map-based or video format, at least not yet. Xue has created a video of changes in surface temperature, salinity and currents over a one-month period. For now, we must settle for maps and videos that represent a slice of the bay rather than its full, four-dimensional reality.

Numerical models of natural systems are notoriously imperfect. Was the data used to build the model collected in the right places, at the right times? How important are the finer scale currents? The currents change from season to season, but do they also change from day to day or week to week?

As data are added to the model it will become more robust. The next step in building the model is to incorporate the satellite data, a process called "data assimilation." The introduction of satellite data into the model will help to improve its accuracy, because of the great volume of data available relative to the very limited hydrographic data record for Penobscot Bay. Although the satellite only "sees" the surface, and in big chunks at that, it takes in all of it (except on cloudy days), several times a day.

The model, in turn, will help provide a link between the data on sea surface temperature, captured by satellite, and the data from below the surface, collected by buoys and on research vessels.

arch cruises. Today, we can at best say that the information provided by analysis of satellite data is consistent with the hydrographic data collected in the field; but it is consistent only when averaged over several weeks or more. On a day-to-day basis there appears to be little connection between the two data sources. Xue hopes to use data assimilation to sharpen the model and use it to probe for answers about this apparent discontinuity. The more accurately the model reproduces known oceanographic conditions in the bay; the more it can be used to estimate conditions for points where we have no data.

For now, the model is limited to the physical properties of the Penobscot Bay ecosystem, for two reasons. First, the physical aspects of this ecosystem predominate in determining its workings, and second, the biology of the ecosystem is not yet well enough understood to fit into the model. We understand, generally, how an influx of cold salty water affects the relatively warmer and slightly fresher water of the bay in summer, for example, but we really don't know much about how the bay's food web functions.

The first foray into adding biology to the model will be incorporating the wealth of lobster data collected by the project. These data include information linking the various life stages of the lobster to physical parameters of the ecosystem, such as sediment and bottom type, temperature, salinity and currents. Although we understand that lobsters are scavengers, that large fish such as striped bass and cod are

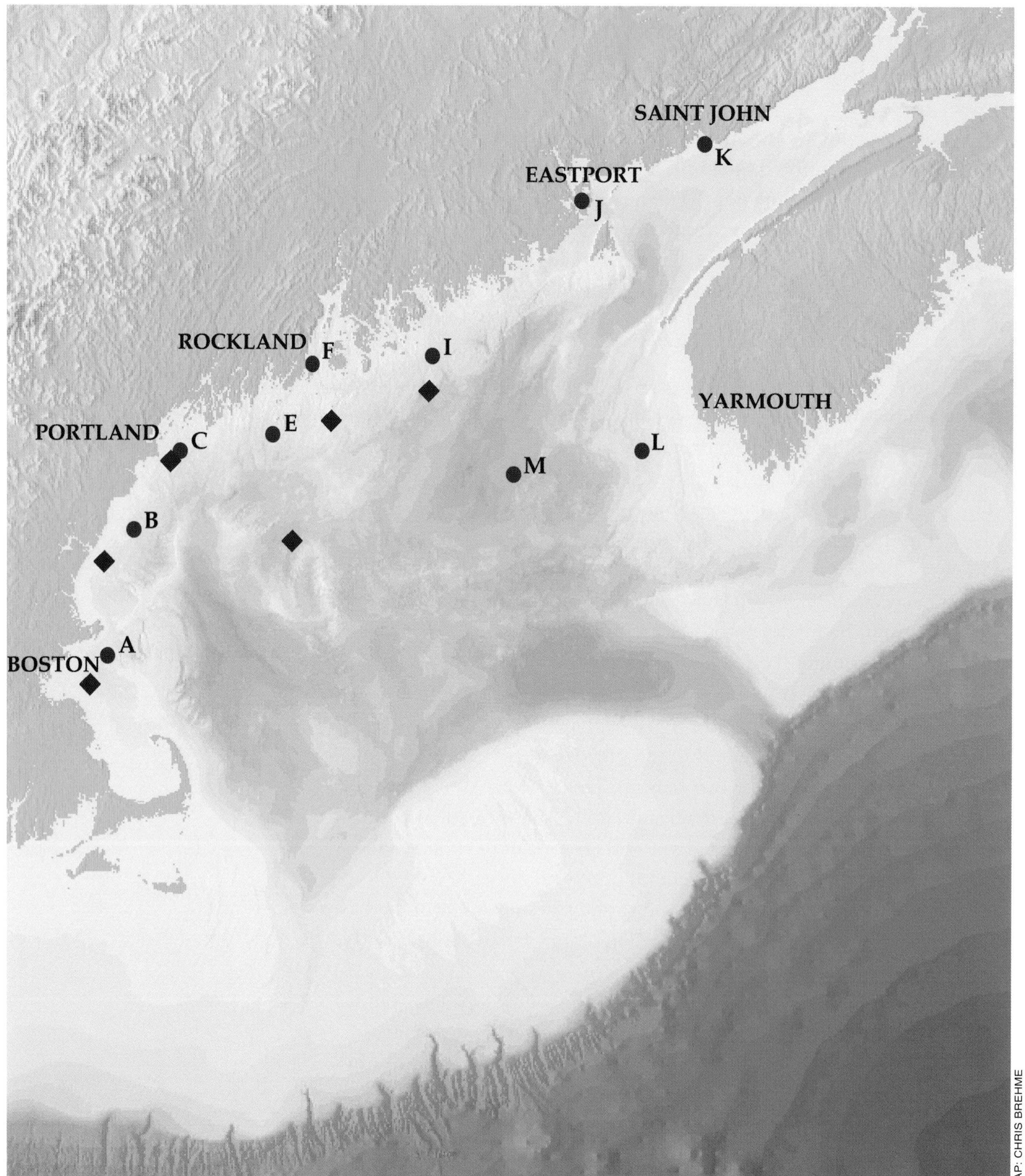

GoMOOS and NOAA buoy array in the Gulf of Maine now report sea conditions every hour from the website www.gomoos.org.

known to prey on lobster, we don't know enough about these relationships to build them into the model. Further complicating the picture are human-induced changes in the ecosystem. Perhaps most important, from the perspective of fisheries management, we don't know enough about the relationship between abundance at the larval stage and level of recruitment into the fishery as these larvae mature.

Xue and Incze are collaborating to use the model to simulate the potential pathways of larvae by interjecting particles into the model at various locations and depths and tracking their trajectories over a period of time equivalent to larval development, which depends on the temperature.

In one sense, because it is based on field data, the model is being developed and tested looking backwards. The goal, once the model is completed, is to use it to look forward, to predict a range of possibilities for how the bay may behave in the future. Based on what we know about how Penobscot Bay has functioned in the past, what can we say about how it will function in the future? If the bit of the life of the system that we've chosen as the starting point for building our model is "typical" then we will be able to predict how the system will function on average over a fairly long period of time but not necessarily how it will respond on any given day.

Predictive models are tricky; accurately modeling past conditions within an ecosystem by no means guarantees that the model can predict the future - it's a little bit like driving your car by looking in the rear-view mirror. A certain degree of randomness withik of conditions that might prevail in the future. For Penobscot Bay's lobster fishery, however, predictions of even a range of the harvest that fishermen could expect would be a boon to managers and fishermen alike. A predictive model would also help with other management issues, such as estimating pollution impacts from land-based discharges and floating fish pens, calculating the trajectory of an oil spill, understanding the distribution of toxic red tides, and identifying locations for collecting wild shellfish spat for use in enhancement projects.

GoMOOS The Penobscot Bay Collaborative has contributed to the development of the Gulf of Maine Ocean Observing System (GoMOOS).

The use of automated data buoys for applied research in Penobscot Bay coincided with a growth in interest in a source of long-term data on oceanographic conditions in the Gulf of Maine. Such knowledge provides a context for data collected over a shorter period of time; without it, it can be difficult to judge the significance of the shorter-term data set. Several months of planning resulted in the design of a monitoring system which,

MAP: CHRIS BREHME

Surface current coverage area from new GoMOOS shore based radar stations

The circulation model that is an integral part of the Penobscot Bay Collaborative's work allows many different kinds of experiments to be run to test different scenarios. In the map at left , seven "particles" (points simulating larvae) were released in the surface waters of Eastern Maine Coastal Current trend along the coast, but none enter the bay. However, particles (or larvae) traveling near the bottom of the water column in a model run (right) do enter West Penobscot Bay. Experiments such as these suggest to scientists that larvae in surface waters will have difficulty entering the bay, but those lower in the water column may ride the currents well up into the bay.

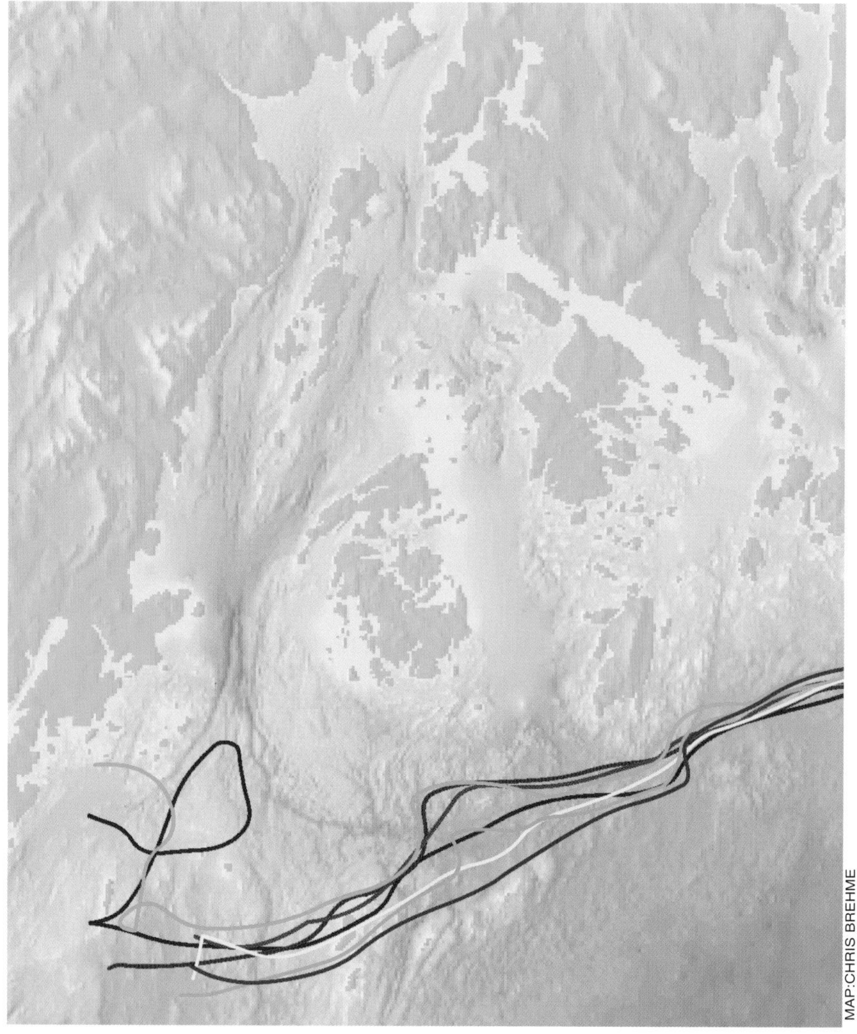

MAP:CHRIS BREHME

having started with the example of the Penobscot Bay Collaborative, was expanded to include much of the Gulf of Maine as well as several new kinds of sensors. These include a type of land-based radar that provides data on surface currents and sensors that detect light levels and the presence of chlorophyll, the essential chemical in plant life. Funded by the federal government, GoMOOS became operational in the summer of 2001 with a dozen buoys simultaneously sending "real-time" data back to shore to be broadcast on the Internet. Intended as a data utility and not as a research project, the goal of GoMOOS is to provide data to those who need detailed and real-time information on what's happening in the Gulf of Maine. Such data are tremendously valuable to a

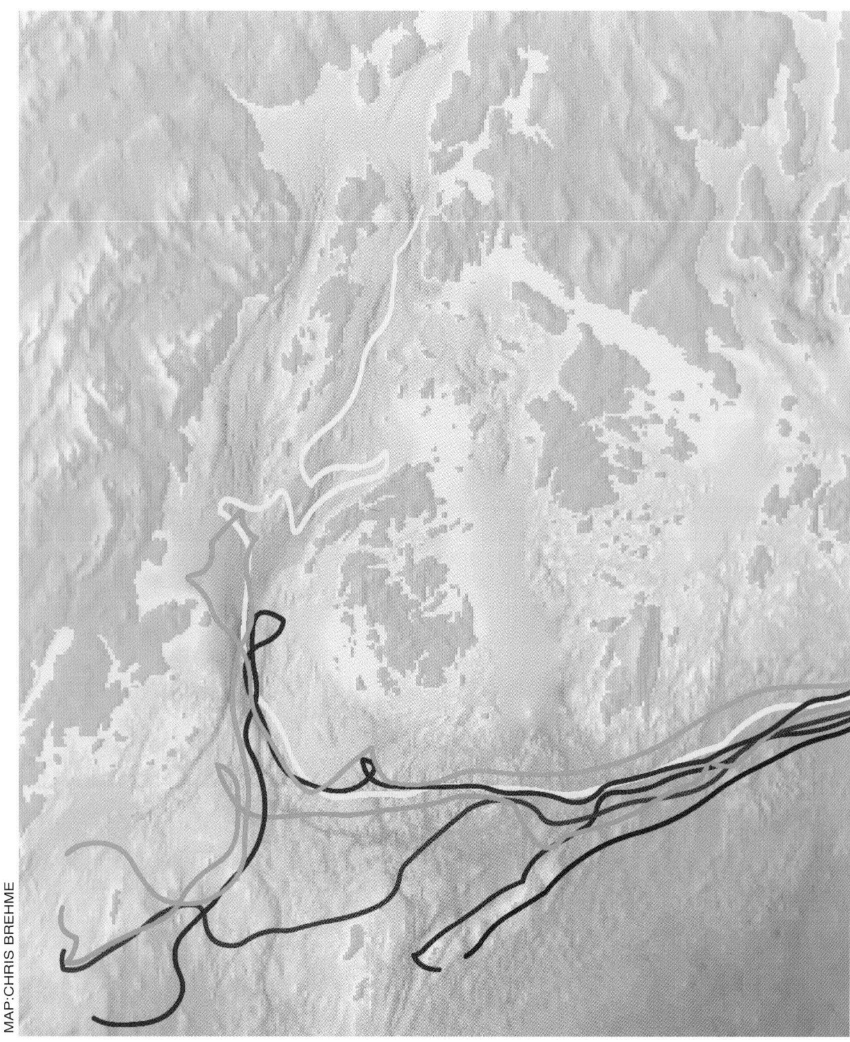

MAP:CHRIS BREHME

great number of users of the marine environment. Nested together, the Penobscot Bay Collaborative, GoMOOS and a national network of monitoring systems will allow for analysis of ecosystems at several different scales.

PETER RALSTON

8

Learning New Languages

TOWARD A NEW SYSTEM FOR MANAGING LOBSTERS

THIS BOOK HAS told the story of collaborative field research since 1996, in Penobscot Bay and the waters that circulate through it. For the past five years the diverse members and participants in the Penobscot Bay Collaborative have worked to develop new channels of communication and scientific methods that may one day enable managers and fishermen to predict future harvests. The Collaborative has succeeded in demonstrating that cooperation among previous antagonists is a highly effective means—perhaps the only means—of advancing the scientific enterprise in marine fisheries. In the most fundamental sense, the Collaborative has served as a meeting ground where fishermen, scientists and managers can understand one another better.

Lobstermen and scientists are beginning to learn how to talk to one another and to share information from very different perspectives. There is a sea change underway along the Maine coast as improved channels of communication develop. The stakes for improving the dialog are high since no one wants to imagine what the Maine coast would be like without lobsters or the communities that depend on them.

Members of these groups almost speak mutually unintelligible languages. Scientists are expected to speak with careful and measured accuracy about what is precisely known. Fishermen speak about what they see on a day-to-day basis on their fishing grounds, which are small parts of larger systems such as Penobscot Bay or the Gulf of Maine. And finally, managers speak of the decisions that must be made over wide areas, under the intense pressure of deadlines with conflicting information, regardless of the actual state of knowledge.

Changing the Rules How has this scientific endeavor influenced management decisions that regulate the harvest of lobsters, and how will it continue to affect those decisions in the future?

In recent years divers have begun to study lobsters in their own habitat rather than rely solely on observations from laboratory study.

NICK CALOYIANIS

For most of the first 125 years of state lobster management, the Maine Legislature made all the formal rules. Lobstermen enforced plenty of informal "rules" through trap wars, violence and the threat of it, but ultimate authority resided in Augusta—and, to an increasing degree, in Washington through the decisions of the National Marine Fisheries Service.

During the past 15 years, as lobsters became more and more plentiful and other marine fisheries were depleted, an increasing number of fishermen entered the lobster fishery, using more and more gear, going further and further offshore during ever lengthening fishing seasons. During the mid-to-late 1990s, fishermen deployed more than two million lobster traps in Maine waters. Lobstermen complained about an "arms race," in which larger numbers of traps were fished by ever faster and more expensive boats. Some lobster boats out of Portland fished between 3,000 and 4,000 traps apiece. In Penobscot Bay, the most aggressive lobstermen began fishing 2,000 traps. "Fishermen were caught in a competitive spiral just to stay in the game," noted one observer.

In 1995, under the leadership of Maine's first woman Commissioner or Marine Resources, Robin Alden, and with the backing of the state's independent governor, Angus King, the legislature adopted the first-ever statewide trap limit. The new law capped the number of traps an individual lobsterman could fish at 1,200, and that number would be stepped down over a five-year period to a maximum of 800 traps. A little-recognized provision of this same legislation had an even more significant impact on the way lobsters are managed: it created seven separate lobster manage-

Robin Alden

"FISHERIES SCIENCE HASN'T BEEN CURIOUS ENOUGH."

CHRIS AYRES

"Top-down laws sap the sense of responsibility from the people being regulated," says Robin Alden, a fisheries consultant based in Stonington. "Regulations need to come from the people interacting with the resource." This statement may sound surprising, coming from a former Commissioner of the Maine Department of Marine Resources (DMR), the state agency charged with overseeing commercial fisheries in state waters, but Alden is a firm believer in requiring management responsibility of a natural resource from the people that depend on it the most: the fishermen. "The lobster zone law is a large scale experiment in decentralizing responsibility for fishery management decisions. This is unique in the nation, and, in fact, anywhere in the world," says Alden.

Alden has been a voice for the fishing community since the early 1970s when she was working for the local newspaper in Stonington, and realized that there was not enough being written about the fishing industry. She began writing about area clammers and became aware of the accumulated knowledge of local fishermen, and the disconnect between them and regulators. Soon she saw the need for a continuous forum for fisheries issues, and founded *Maine Commercial Fisheries*, a newspaper dedicated to covering the fishing industry, in 1973. The name was later changed to *Commercial Fisheries News*, and Alden served as its publisher and editor.

Gov. Angus King appointed Alden DMR Commissioner in 1995, and she served three years. During this time she was instrumental in the passage of the Maine Lobster Zone Management Law, which gave lobstermen a voice in the management process.

Since serving as DMR Commissioner, Alden has helped found, and is currently co-chair of the Stonington Fisheries Alliance, a citizens group that supports grass-roots fisheries organizations around the Gulf of Maine. She is also an independent fisheries consultant and works to bring the scientific community and the fishing industry closer together. As DMR Commissioner Alden supported the Penobscot Bay Collaborative. She notes that fisheries science is usually performed on a very large scale and mainly involves quantifying biomass. This approach necessarily ignores local, fine-scale ecological and fisheries behavior characteristics—the type of information that fishermen have.

"Fisheries science as applied to fisheries management hasn't been curious enough," Alden says. "In contrast, this project generated as many new questions as answers, and has given fisheries science a jolt."

(BN)

SCRIBNER'S MONTHLY, JUNE 1881

ment zones along the Maine coast.

In 1997, with the election of councils in each of the local zones by lobster license holders, new regulations began to change important features of the fishery. Six of the seven Lobster Zone Councils responded over the next few years by enacting lower lobster trap limits than the state maximum. By 2001, the majority of Lobster Zone Councils also adopted additional regulations to limit entry into the lobster fishery—a significant conservation management measure.

Atlantic States Marine Fisheries Commission While Maine was delegating more and more authority to manage lobsters to the local level in a Jeffersonian experiment in local self-governance, another major shift occurred in the way lobsters were managed in federal waters. Responsibility for lobster management decisions here was placed in the hands of the Atlantic States Marine Fisheries Commission (ASMFC), a body made up of representatives from different states along the Atlantic Coast. The commission adopts rules that encourage consistency throughout the range of the species. For lobsters, this means that representatives from Maine to Virginia meet to develop harvesting rules that will apply from state to state.

While Maine's three members of the ASMFC are heavily outnumbered by their counterparts from other states, this interstate body has adopted new rules governing the harvest of lobsters throughout their range. Oversized broodstock and V-notched females are now protected in all states and federal waters where a commercial lobster fishery exists—two protections long sought by Maine lobstermen.

These new rules, pioneered in Maine, were adopted elsewhere, over the objections of many parochial interests and jealousies, in large part because Maine's Department of Marine Resources had invested in developing the scientific data to demonstrate their conservation value.

Can Future Lobster Harvests Be Predicted? For most of the duration of the Collaborative, the scientific goal has been to link the dynamics of the Penobscot Bay-Eastern Maine oceanographic system to the biology of different stages of a lobster's life cycle. A detailed understanding of these mechanisms, linking the physical environment to the biology of lobsters, could be called an ecosystem-based model. While the Penobscot Bay Collaborative has not yet produced even a miniaturized version of a model with the power to predict the future abundance of adults (one is being developed, but has not been published), this remarkable collaboration is edging ever closer to a "predictive" model that can withstand the scrutiny of time—the holy grail of all fisheries management.

Much work remains to be done. But there is, at least, the tantalizing outline of a working, conceptual model. Members of the Collaborative have succeeded in describing how the oceanographic currents of the Eastern Maine Coastal Current interact with the currents of Penobscot Bay to drive the major gyre-like features of the circulation system there. Members have also discovered the pattern of oceanographic temperature fronts in the region of Penobscot Bay, which are likely in the long run to be useful in understanding the distribution of many species, not just

Over 144 harbors from an equal number of towns along the Maine coast harvest commercial quantities of lobsters and have for over 150 years.

Lobstermen have become increasingly sophisticated in the gear they need to remain successful in this highly competitive industry. The size of their investments in their boat, gear and technology makes their margin for error very narrow.

PETER RALSTON

lobsters.

The many lobstermen who have participated in the Department of Marine Resources' expanded sea sampling program have contributed greatly to an understanding of the locations of broodstock female lobsters. Others, including fishermen, have mapped "hot" and "cold" spots of lobster settlement and linked these observations to similar patterns of juvenile lobsters found in lobstermen's traps.

Members of the Collaborative have reliably and repeatedly located and described the earliest stage of larval lobsters shortly after they hatch from eggs carried by broodstock lobsters. This same group has also successfully located and described the last stages of the larval life cycle, just before they settle to the bottom for the beginning of their benthic lives. But questions about the whereabouts of the middle two stages of larval lobsters and the fundamental link between settlement and harvestable lobsters remain unanswered.

Time and adequate resources will help solve these mysteries. Meanwhile, an understanding of the relative contributions of distant broodstock and sources of

Leroy Bridges

"WE ARE THE STEWARDS OF THIS RESOURCE"

Leroy Bridges fishes for lobsters year-round out of Sunshine, on Deer Isle. Lobstering has been his way of life for the past 24 years, and he hopes that will continue long into the future. Bridges has been active within the fishing industry and in cooperation with the scientific community. A former president of the Downeast Lobstermen's Association, he was instrumental in testing and improving an electronic logbook for lobstermen called the HMS-140, from Thistle Marine. These logbooks are now being used by 124 lobstermen from around the state to provide valuable information about the lobster population to the Maine Department of Marine Resources.

DEBORAH DUBRULE

When the Penobscot Bay Collaborative was brought to his attention, Bridges volunteered to take sea samplers out with him, and even allowed his boat to be used as a dive platform for a study involving juvenile lobster abundance. He believes most lobstermen are willing to take an active role in lobster research.

"We are the stewards of this resource," he says. "Our aim is not to go out and catch the last lobster, we want to ensure a healthy lobster population for generations to come."

Bridges believes cooperation between scientists and fishermen is critical to gathering the best possible data on the resource. Sea sampling allows scientists to see exactly what the lobstermen have been seeing, and where their view on the status of the lobster population comes from. "This type of data collection provides a more complete picture of the real status of the resource, compared to trawl surveys or dockside sampling," Bridges says.

(BN)

local production and retention remains elusive.

What is Ecosystem Management? The Magnuson-Stevens or Sustainable Fisheries Act is the federal law governing the harvest of all marine species that live or move through federal waters, beyond the three-mile limit of state jurisdiction and out to the 200-mile limit of federal authority.

The Magnuson-Stevens Act must be reauthorized in the near future by Congress. A key political question is whether the law will require new ecosystem-based management approaches to fisheries regulation. Ecosystem-based management, in which a species is considered in relationship to its physical environment and to predator-prey interactions, has become common in the management of terrestrial wildlife. But in fisheries management, this approach is still elusive. With so many stocks of the nation's fisheries in a depleted state, there is a great deal of political pressure, from both environmentalists and fishermen, to find better ways of managing fisheries.

It may not be possible, for example, to maximize the harvest of both a predator and its prey at the same time. If cod and haddock both feed on certain sizes of herring at different stages of their development, fishing for herring at the same time and place may work against increasing the harvests of cod and haddock. Or if herring are fished intensively near areas that support seabirds and marine mammals that also feed on herring, the result can be unintended population reductions of non-target species.

On the other hand, lobster abundance may be controlled by oceanographic conditions beyond the control of fisheries managers. So long as older broodstock lobsters are protected, the number of intermediate lobsters harvested may not have a large effect on future population numbers. We need to know what factor or factors control marine populations, and adjust our management strategies accordingly. This is the goal of ecosystem-based fishery management.

Building A Bridge to the Future Maine lobstermen, scientists and managers have adopted various strategies to protect egg-bearing females and large broodstock. In "classical" sustainable-yield management, such strategies tend to be ignored. Yet Maine's lobster management strategies appear to be working.

The Penobscot Bay Collaborative has focused on finding and analyzing the patterns of distribution and abundance of the various life stages of the lobster, in different portions of its geographic range. To improve the understanding of the pat-

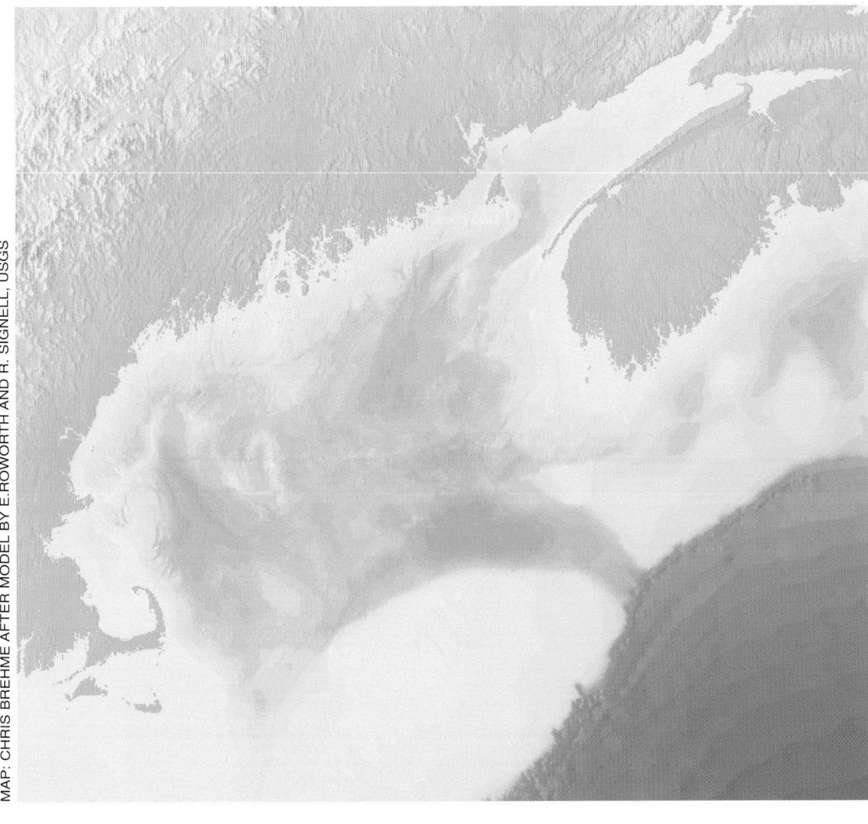
MAP: CHRIS BREHME AFTER MODEL BY E.ROWORTH AND R. SIGNELL, USGS

The Gulf of Maine is an ecologically complex place that fisheries scientists need to understand better if we are to improve the management of the region's diverse and valuable marine resources.

terns that have been observed along the Maine coast requires understanding how oceanography affects different lobster life stages, as well as appreciating which stages depend on which particular marine habitats.

The Collaborative has demonstrated that finer-scale ecological information is essential to anticipating lobster population changes in the years ahead. There are still holes in these ideas, some of them very large. We need to know what portions of the lobster population are reproducing, and where the eggs are hatching out. We need to know whether the number of lobster eggs produced varies from year to year. We need to know where the eggs are released—if they are released in deep water offshore, the results will be different than if eggs are released in shallow waters up in the bays. The delivery of lobster larvae to nursery grounds can vary a great deal from year to year if they are hatching in different places, even if the oceanography and currents don't.

NICK CALOYIANIS

In six of Maine's seven lobster zones, lobstermen have voted to reduce the number of traps they put in the water. Another five zones have voted to limit the number of new fishermen to enter the fishery in an effort to conserve the resource.

At the very least, everyone from the most skeptical lobsterman to the most eager scientist is beginning to agree on the value of ongoing monitoring of broodstock locations from sea sampling. And everyone agrees that monitoring larval lobster numbers in order to develop an annual index may help explain abundance in the years ahead.

The Penobscot Bay Collaborative has asked questions that must be answered if, as and when the management of our fisheries shifts toward more of an ecosystem-based approach. The shift toward ecosystem-based approaches will not rely on one primary index such as a trawl survey, but should be based on multiple indices of abundance from different life stages. The logic of using multiple indices is simple: the marine environment is so complex and our understanding of the sea is still so primitive that for the indefinite future, uncertainty will be the dominant scientific posture toward any question regarding the status of important stocks. To reduce uncertainty, therefore, we must figure out cost effective means of sampling several different signals of a species' abundance or decline. A rapidly changing marine environment is extremely difficult to understand, and no single index will provide what we need, in order to know what is manageable and what is not.

Working with fishermen, managers and scientists are close to developing the predictive models that have always eluded them. If they are found to be reliable, these predictions could help, for example, inform a lobsterman in deciding whether to invest in more gear or a bigger boat—or to wait until conditions appear more favorable. They can also help distinguish between changes caused by natural factors, and changes due to fishing and management practices.

Separating Nature From the Hand of Man A few years ago at the annual Maine Fisherman's Forum, where fishermen and scientists have been gathering once a year to share information, an oceanographer was asked to lead a discussion on the North Atlantic Oscillation. Although less well known than its Pacific counterpart, El Nino, the North Atlantic Oscillation is a sea-sawing atmospheric pattern that drives ocean currents and circulation throughout the entire North Atlantic Basin. For us, this oscillation results in either warmer or cooler ocean temperatures entering the Gulf of Maine in the late winter and early spring. A fisherman looking at the peaks and valleys of the temperatures collected over many decades remarked, "That graph looks like my revenue during the last 20 years."

In an era when so many fisheries resources are intensely exploited throughout all oceans of the globe, we tend to focus on overfishing as the major cause of fisheries decline and fishermen as the major culprit. This is a vast oversimplification. Certainly overfishing is a serious and chronic problem in many fisheries that can lead to a cascade of largely unpredictable effects throughout the marine ecosystem. But the Maine lobster fishery, which has been accused of being chronically overfished for the past two decades has been resilient, even robust. The information collected by the members and participants in the Penobscot Bay Collaborative indicates that still poorly understood oceanographic factors, operating over large areas, drive the delivery of eggs and larvae to coastal nursery areas, determining abundance on a year to year basis. If fisheries managers had cut fishing effort on Maine's lobster resource during the past five years as many had advocated, it is not at all clear that a more sustainable fishery would have resulted.

It is important that we develop ways of sorting out the effects of the hand of man from the ever-changing natural pulses and rhythms of the ocean. Otherwise we will never be able to distinguish between outcomes we can influence —perhaps even manage—from those that we cannot.

Marine Protected Areas One of the most reasonable strategies that would enable us to distinguish between the local effects of fishing activities and oceanographic or pollution stresses on the marine ecosystem would be to set aside parts of the sea as baseline areas. Called "marine protected areas," these no-take zones for fishing or other extractive activities have been vehemently opposed by virtually all fishermen throughout the Gulf of Maine region. It's not hard to see why. Fishing has been a way of life along the Maine coast for nearly 400 years and there is hardly a square foot of the ocean bottom or a cubic foot of the water column that is not fished by someone for something during the course of a year. Ceding control of even a fraction of this proud patrimony runs against the grain.

Nevertheless, the larger threat to fishing families and communities comes from our ignorance of the basic forces that control fish abundance. Until we can distinguish the difference between the forces we can manage and those we cannot, fishermen risk being cast as society's problem rather than as what the lobstermen of Penobscot Bay have surely become: marine stewards of the bay.

PETER RALSTON

additional reading

Acheson, James M. 1988. *The Lobster Gangs of Maine*. Hanover, NH: University Press of New England.

Conkling, Philip W. 1998. Layer by layer, Penobscot Bay reveals itself: The great lobster collaboration. *Island Journal,* 17.

Cowan, Diane F. 1999. Method for assessing relative abundance, size-distribution, and growth of recently settled and early juvenile lobster (Homarus americanus) in the lower intertidal zone. *Journal of Crustacean Biology,* 19 (4).

Dickson, Stephen M. 1999. *Penobscot Bay 10,000 years ago,* [Online]. Available: http://www.state.me.us/doc/nrimc/mgs/sites-1999/may99.htm.

Factor, Jan R. (ed.). 1995. *Biology of the Lobster*: Homarus americanus. New York: Academic Press.

Island Institute. 1998. *Penobscot Bay Marine Resource Collaborative*, [Online]. Available: http://www.penbay.net.

Island Institute and National Oceanic and Atmospheric Administration, National Environmental Satellite Data and Information Service. 2002. *Lobsters: From fishermen to satellites,* [CD-ROM interactive exhibit]. Available: Island Institute, 386 Main St., Rockland, Me.

Island Institute, Mainewatch Institute and Compass Light Productions. 2001. *Fishing for the Future* [Video]. Available: Island Institute, Archipelago, 386 Main St., Rockland, Me, 04841.

Lazzari, Mark. 2001. Dynamics of larval fish abundance in Penobscot Bay, Maine. *Fishery Bulletin* 99.

Lazzari, Mark and Tupper, Ben. 2002. Importance of shallow water habitats for demersal fishes and decapod crustaceans in Penobscot Bay, Maine. *Environmental Biology of Fishes* 63 (1).

MacDonald, William and Hayden, Anne. 1998. Maine's embayments: Forming integral connections between land and sea. Habitat, *Journal of the Maine Audubon Society*, 15 (4), 30-35.

Maine Office of GIS. 1998. *Penobscot Bay Project data*, [Online]. Available: http://apollo.ogis.state.me.us/projects/penobay/penobay/htm.

Martin, Kenneth R. and Lipfert, Nathan R. 1985. *Lobstering and the Maine Coast*. Bath, Me: Maine Maritime Museum.

National Oceanic and Atmospheric Administration, Coastal Services Center. 2000. *Using remote sensing to add coastal management issues: The Maine project,* [CD-ROM]. Available: NOAA Coastal Services Center, 2234 South Hobson Ave., Charleston, S.C. 29905-2413.

Palma, A. T., Steneck, Robert. S. and Wilson, Carl J. 1999. Settlement-driven, multiscale demographic patterns of large benthic decapods in the Gulf of Maine. *J. Exp. Mar. Biol. Ecol.* 241: 107-136.

Steneck, Robert S. 1997. Fisheries-induced biological changes to the structure and function of the Gulf of Maine ecosystem. Plenary paper. In Wallace, G. T., and Braasch, E. F. (eds). *Proceedings of the Gulf of Maine Ecosystem Dynamics Scientific Symposium and Workshop*. Regional Association for Research on the Gulf of Maine. Hanover, NH, RARGOM Report, 91 - 1.

Steneck, Robert. S. In press 2002. Are we overfishing the American lobster? Some biological perspectives. In Buchsbaum, Robinson and Peterson (eds). *Decline of Fisheries Resources in New England: Evaluating the Impact of Overfishing, Contamination and Habitat Degradation.* Cambridge, Mass.: MIT Press.

Steneck, Robert. S. and Carlton, James. T. 2001. Human alterations of marine communities: Students beware! In Bertness, M, Gaines, S., and Hay, M. (eds). *Marine Community Ecology*. Sunderland, Mass.: Sinauer Press.

Steneck, Robert S. and Wilson, Carl. J. 2001. Long-term and large scale spatial and temporal patterns in demography and landings of the American lobster, Homarus americanus, in Maine. *Journal of Marine and Freshwater Research*. 52: 1302 - 1319.

Thomas, Andrew; Byrne, Deirdre and Weatherbee, Ryan. In press 2002. Coastal sea surface temperature variability from Landsat infrared data. *Remote Sensing of the Environment*, 81.

Xue, Huijie, Xu, Yu, Brooks, David, Pettigrew, Neal R. and Wallinga, John. 2000. Modeling the circulation in Penobscot Bay, Maine. In *Estuarine and Coastal Modeling – Proceedings of the 6th International Conference on Estuarine and Coastal Modeling*.

acknowledgements

The following fishermen and others participated in sea sampling and assisted the Penobscot Bay Project in other ways. The list is long, but surely incomplete. Our apologies to anyone inadvertently left off.

Robin Adair, Peter Aiken, Mark Allen, Lewis Alley, Ron Alley, Shirley Alley, Tim Alley, Mark Ames, Pete Ames, Troy Ames, Eric Anderson, Herman Anderson Jr., Jerry Andrews, Lee Arey, James Ashey, Jackie Backman, Junior Backman, Ralph Backman, Bob Baines, Jack Baines, Bill Barter, Brian Barter, Jason Barter, Chris Bates, Barry Baudanza, Dale Beal, Jeff Beal, Mitchell Beal, Charles Begin, Dave Benner, Devin Benner, David Berry, Brian Bickford, Jonathan Bickford, Lewis Bishop, David Black, David Black, Bob Blanchard, Doug Boynton, James Brackett, Norman Brackett, Robert Bracy, Earl Brewer, George Brewer, Mardsen Brewer, Russell Brewer, Dick Bridges, Leroy Bridges, Ernie Burgess

Lewis Cameron, Greg Canning, Jon Carter, Ralph Carter, Scott Carter, Dwight Carver, Mark Carver, James Chalmers, Daniel Cheney, Eric Churchill, Gordon Connell, Earl Cooper, Dave Cousens, Craig Crowley, Larry Crowley, Kip Crute, Bruce Damon, Dan Davis, Jason Day, Walter Day, Doug Demellier, Gerald Doughty, Lawrence Durfee, Randy Durkee, Justin Dyer, Shannon Dyer, Gregg Eaton, Jim Eaton, Jonathan Elwell, Rob Eugley, Tony Eugley, Bob Eugley Sr., Sid Farren, Patrice Farrey, Gary Farrin, Gordon Farrin, Ken Farrin, Bruce Farrin Jr., Bruce Fernald, Mark Fernald, Chuck Fuller

Adam Gamage, Greg Gamage, Arnold Gamage Jr., Arnold Gamage Sr., Wayne Gilbert, Dusty Goodwin, Frank Gotwals, Eugene Gove, Jim Greenlaw, Bob Hallinan, Kurt Hallowell, Travis Harriman, Roger Haskell, Richard Hill, David Hiltz Jr., Ken Holbrook, Mike Hutchings, Archie Hutchinson, Gene Hutchinson, Melvin Hutchinson, Steve Hutchinson, Jamie Johnson, Steve Johnson, Brent Jones, Eric Jones, Jeff Jones, Nathan Jones, Bill Kelsey, Lewis Kelsey, Arnold Kinney, Bill Kirby III, Alan Knowlton, Omer Lagasse, George Lane, Perlie Lane, Russell Lane Jr., Thomas Lawson, Craig Lazaro, Richard Lermond, Wayne Lessner, Troy Lewis, Bill Libby, Oscar Look III, Jim Lowe, Dick Lowell, Dan Lunt

Dan MacDonald, Jack MacDonald, David MacMahan, Earl MacVane, Tom MacVane, Stuart Mahan, David Mahonen II, Lawrence Marriner, Joseph McGuire, Brian McLain, William McLain, Teddy McLaughlin, Donald McMahan Jr., Sonny McVane, Jack Merrill, John Merrill III, Keith Miller, Tom Moody, Casey Morrill, Malcolm Morrill, Bruce Morton, Harold Morton Sr., Dan Murdock, John Murdock, Shawn Murray, Mike Myriek, Russell Nisbet Jr., Anson Norton, David Norton, Jeff Norwood, Robert Norwood, Larry Nystrom, Jim O'Brien, Robert O'Hara, Richard Olson, Richard Osgood Jr.

Donn Page, Mark Page, Philip Page, Lee Pappianne, Frank Peasley, Jeff Peterson, Randy Philbrook, Mike Pinkham, Orman Poland, Carl Prentice, Greg Prior, Bob Putnam, David Rice, Walter Rich, Victor Richards, Todd Ritchie, Steve Robbins III, Roman Rozenski, Greg Runge, Francis Seiders, John Seiders, George Sewall, Michael Shepard, Wesley Shute, Adam Simmons, Albert Simmons, Brian Simmons, Keith Simmons, Richard Simmons, Steve Simmons, Tim Simmons, Harold Simmons II, Malcolm Small, Al Smith, Jay Smith, Kendall Smith, Ken Spear, Eddy Spencer, Sherm Stanley, Sherman Stanley, Dan Staples, Bunk Stone, Charles Stone III

David Taylor, Frank Thompson, John Thompson, Matthew Thompson, Matt Thomson, Paul Thormann, David Tibbets, Cortland Tolman, Bill Tomkins, Steve Train, Jim Tripp, John Tripp, Mike Tripp, Danny Trundy, Rick Trundy, Paul Venno, Troy Wadleigh, John Wallace, Mark Wallace, Rick Walsh, Bobby Warren, Ernest Warren, Erik Waterman, Albert Westhaver, Bill Whitcomb Jr., Pat White, Paul Wiegleb, Walter Willey IV, John Williams, Tim Winchenbach, Bert Witham, Chris Young, Wayne Young, Mike Yurchick, Zoe Zanidakis, Dominic Zanke

The following funding sources were instrumental in leveraging additional grants and support following the lead commitment of NOAA's National Environmental Satellite Data and Information Service:

Private Foundations: Branta Foundation, Comer Foundation, Chichester du Pont Foundation, Davis Conservation Foundation, Fore River Foundation, Foundation for Marine Sciences, Island Foundation, MBNA Education Foundation, Maine Outdoor Heritage Fund, Maine Community Foundation, The Pew Charitable Trusts, David Rockefeller Fund, Surdna Foundation, Henry P. Kendall Foundation, and Virginia Wellington Cabot Foundation.

Institutional Support: Bigelow Laboratory, Island Institute, Maine Coastal Program of the State Planning Office, National Sea Grant Program, National Undersea Research Program, NOAA's Coastal Zone Management Program, Northeast Consortium and University of Maine.

The authors would like to acknowledge the special contributions of the late Maureen Keller, Bigelow Laboratory for Ocean Sciences, to the first two years of the Penobscot Bay Collaborative. Dr. Keller passed away in 1999 before the project was completed.

The following research scientists participated in the Collaborative:
Brian Beal from ***Beals Island Regional Shellfish Hatchery***:
Mike Dunnington, Cynthia Erickson, Lewis Incze, Peter Larsen, David Phinney, Richard Wahle, Nicholas Wolff, Charles Yentsch from ***Bigelow Laboratory for Ocean Sciences***;
Diane Cowan, Sara Ellis from ***The Lobster Conservancy***;
Richard Langton, Mark Lazzari, Linda Mercer, Carl Wilson from ***Maine Department of Marine Resources***:
Stephen Dickson from ***Maine Department of Conservation/NRIMC-Geology***;
John Barlow, Barry Kilch; Andy McLeod and Pamela Schreiner from ***Maine Maritime Academy***;
Larry Harwood, David Kirouac, Daniel Walters from ***Maine Office of GIS***;
Paul Anderson from ***Maine Sea Grant Program***;
David Brooks from ***Texas A&M University***;
Eric Annis, Deirdre Byrne, Yong Chen, Joseph Kelley, Linda Mangum, Neal Pettigrew, Robert Steneck, Andrew Thomas, John Wallinga, Ryan Weathebee, Huijie Xue; from ***University of Maine School of Marine Sciences***; and lead interns Damien Drisco and Greg Welch from ***Darling Marine Center***:
Guy Meadows and Hans Van Sumeren from ***University of Michigan, Dept. of Naval Architecture & Marine Engineering***:
Peter Cornillon and, Shakeela Baker from ***University of Rhode Island, Graduate School of Oceanography***;

The following served as members of the Maine State Advisory Committee
Seth Barker, Penn Estabrook, George Lapointe, John Sowles from ***Maine Department of Marine Resources***;
Lee Doggett from ***Maine Department of Environmental Protection***;
Susan White from ***Maine Department of Marine Resources***;
Robert Marvinney from ***Maine State Dept. of Conservation, Natural Resources Information & Mapping Center***;
Kathleen Leyden, Josie Quintrell (Committee chair) from ***Maine State Planning Office***;

Other Contributors:
Leroy Bridges, ***Downeast Lobsterman's Association;***
Stephen Miller, ***Islesboro Island Trust***;
David Cousens, Patrice Farrey, Pat White, ***Maine Lobstermen's Association***;
Richard Arnold, ***Thistle Marine, LLD;***
Robin Alden, Ted Ames, ***Stonington Fishermen's Alliance***;
Stewart Fefer, ***U.S. Fish and Wildlife Service, Gulf of Maine Project***;
Ronald Beard, Esperanza Stancioff, Sherman Hoyt, ***University of Maine Cooperative Extension***;
Kent Kirkpatrick, ***Wells National Estuarine Research Reserve***;
Jeff Dworsky, Nick Caloyianis, David Conover

Federal Agency and Other Advisors:
Peter Colvin, Frank Sadowski, ***ERIM International;***
H. Lee Dantzler, Robert Feden, Jill Meyer, ***NOAA/National Environmental Satellite Data Information Service***;
John Dietz, Christopher Elvidge, ***NOAA/National Geographic Data Center***;
Lori Cary-Kothera, Nicholas Schmidt ***NOAA/Coastal Services Center***;

Island Institute Fellows:
Helen Chabot, Allyson Flauver, Nate Geraldi, Susan Little, Kathleen Reardon, Jessica Stevens

Island Institute Staff, Current and Former
Norene Bishop, Andrew Boyce, Chrisopher Brehme, Christopher Broadway, Christina Cash, Linda Cortright, Scott Dickerson, Leslie Fuller, Sheri Floge, William MacDonald, Nathan Michaud, Annette Naegel, Benjamin Neal, Charles Oldham, David Platt, Peter Ralston, Corrie Roberts, Josee Shelley, Sandra Thomas

Special Thanks to
Leroy Bridges, David Cousens, Walter Day, and Dan Staples.

The Island Institute is a non-profit organization that serves as a voice for the balanced future of the islands and waters of the Gulf of Maine.

We are guided by an island ethic that recognizes the strength and fragility of Maine's island communities and the finite nature of the Gulf of Maine ecosystems.

Along the Maine coast, the Island Institute seeks to support the islands' year round communities; conserve Maine's island and marine biodiversity for future generations; develop model solutions that balance the needs of the coast's cultural and natural communities; provide opportunities for discussion over responsible use of finite resources and provide information to assist competing interests in arriving at constructive solutions.